The Asian Cookbook

Culinary Journeys Through China, Japan, Korea, and Thailand

By Lilly Unis

Introduction

Welcome to "The Asian Cookbook: Culinary Journeys Through China, Japan, Korea, and Thailand." Embark on a gastronomic adventure that celebrates the rich tapestry of Asian cuisine, featuring the distinct flavors, aromas, and traditions of China, Japan, Korea, and Thailand.

Discover the Essence of Chinese Cuisine

In the heart of China, culinary traditions date back thousands of years. From the sizzling streets of Sichuan to the delicate flavors of Cantonese dishes, immerse yourself in the diverse world of Chinese cooking. Explore the harmonious balance of sweet and savory, the mastery of stir-frying, and the art of dim sum, as we uncover the secrets of one of the world's most influential cuisines.

Journey into the Culinary Culture of Japan

Dive into the refined simplicity and artistry of Japanese cuisine. From the umami-rich delights of sushi to the comforting embrace of ramen, each dish reflects a profound connection to nature and seasonality. Uncover the techniques behind delicate sashimi, the meditative process of tea ceremonies, and the soul-warming goodness of a bowl of miso soup. Join us on a culinary pilgrimage through the land of the rising sun.

Explore the Flavors of Korea

Korean cuisine is a captivating blend of bold flavors, vibrant colors, and communal dining. From the fiery depths of kimchi to the sizzling delights of Korean BBQ, savor the complexity of tastes that define this dynamic cuisine. Witness the artistry of banchan, the heartiness of stews, and the thrill of grilling meats at the table. Embark on a journey through the Korean kitchen, where tradition and innovation dance in perfect harmony.

Savor the Spices of Thai Cuisine

Thai cuisine is a symphony of bold and aromatic flavors that dance on the palate. From the tangy delights of tom yum soup to the aromatic allure of green curry, Thai cooking is an exploration of contrasts. Discover the perfect balance of sweet, sour, spicy, and salty in each dish. Learn the art of Thai street food, the secrets of fragrant herbs, and the techniques behind crafting the perfect pad Thai. Let the vibrant and diverse world of Thai cuisine awaken your senses.

In **"The Asian Cookbook,"** we invite you to embrace the culinary diversity of China, Japan, Korea, and Thailand. Whether you're a seasoned home cook or a curious beginner, these pages are a gateway to the flavors and stories that define Asian cuisine. Get ready to embark on a culinary journey that transcends borders and celebrates the magic of Asian cooking.

Table of Contents

Chinese Cuisine

Table of Contents

Japanese Cuisine

Table of Contents

Thai Cuisine

Table of Contents

Korean Cuisine

Chinese Cuisine

General Tso's Chicken

 4 servings   40 Mins   Kcal : 400   Fat: 15g carbs : 40g protein : 25g

General Tso's Chicken is a popular Chinese-American dish known for its sweet and tangy flavor. Crispy chicken bites are coated in a flavorful sauce, creating a delicious balance of textures and tastes.

INGREDIENTS

- 1 pound boneless, skinless chicken thighs, cut into bite-sized pieces
- 1 cup cornstarch
- Vegetable oil for frying
- 2 tablespoons sesame oil
- 3 cloves garlic, minced
- 1 tablespoon ginger, grated
- 1/2 cup soy sauce
- 1/4 cup hoisin sauce
- 1/4 cup rice vinegar
- 3 tablespoons sugar
- 1 teaspoon red pepper flakes (adjust to taste)
- 3 green onions, chopped
- Sesame seeds for garnish

INSTRUCTIONS

1. Dredge chicken pieces in cornstarch, ensuring each piece is well-coated.
2. Heat vegetable oil in a wok or deep pan over medium-high heat. Fry the chicken until golden brown and crispy. Remove and drain on paper towels.
3. In a separate pan, heat sesame oil and sauté garlic and ginger until fragrant.
4. Mix in soy sauce, hoisin sauce, rice vinegar, sugar, and red pepper flakes. Allow the sauce to simmer and thicken.
5. Add the fried chicken to the sauce, tossing to coat evenly.
6. Garnish with chopped green onions and sesame seeds.
7. Serve hot over steamed rice.

Kung Pao Shrimp

 4 servings   30 Mins   Kcal : 350   Fat: 18g carbs : 20g protein : 35g

Kung Pao Shrimp is a classic Chinese stir-fry dish featuring succulent shrimp, crunchy peanuts, and vibrant vegetables in a savory and slightly spicy sauce.

INGREDIENTS

- 1 pound large shrimp, peeled and deveined
- 1/2 cup dry roasted peanuts
- 2 tablespoons vegetable oil
- 3 cloves garlic, minced
- 1 tablespoon ginger, grated
- 1/2 cup diced red bell pepper
- 1/2 cup diced green bell pepper
- 1/2 cup diced zucchini
- 3 green onions, chopped
- 1 tablespoon soy sauce
- 1 tablespoon hoisin sauce
- 1 tablespoon rice vinegar
- 1 teaspoon sugar
- 1 teaspoon red pepper flakes (adjust to taste)
- Cooked rice for serving

INSTRUCTIONS

1. Heat vegetable oil in a wok or skillet over high heat.
2. Stir-fry shrimp until they turn pink and opaque. Remove and set aside.
3. In the same pan, sauté garlic and ginger until aromatic.
4. Add diced bell peppers, zucchini, and green onions. Stir-fry until vegetables are tender-crisp.
5. Return the cooked shrimp to the pan.
6. In a small bowl, mix soy sauce, hoisin sauce, rice vinegar, sugar, and red pepper flakes. Pour the sauce over the shrimp and vegetables.
7. Toss to coat evenly and stir in dry roasted peanuts.
8. Serve hot over cooked rice.

Beef and Broccoli Stir-Fry

 4 servings   25 Mins   Kcal : 320   Fat: 15g carbs : 20g protein : 25g

Beef and Broccoli Stir-Fry is a classic Chinese dish that brings together tender slices of beef, crisp broccoli, and a savory sauce. Quick and easy, it's perfect for a satisfying weeknight meal.

INGREDIENTS

- **1 pound flank steak, thinly sliced**
- **1/4 cup soy sauce**
- **2 tablespoons oyster sauce**
- **1 tablespoon hoisin sauce**
- **1 tablespoon cornstarch**
- **2 tablespoons vegetable oil**
- **3 cups broccoli florets**
- **3 cloves garlic, minced**
- **1 tablespoon ginger, grated**
- **2 green onions, sliced**
- **Cooked white rice for serving**

INSTRUCTIONS

1. In a bowl, marinate sliced beef in soy sauce, oyster sauce, hoisin sauce, and cornstarch for at least 15 minutes.
2. Heat vegetable oil in a wok or skillet over high heat.
3. Stir-fry marinated beef until browned. Remove from the pan.
4. In the same pan, add a bit more oil if needed. Stir-fry broccoli until crisp-tender.
5. Add minced garlic and grated ginger, stirring until fragrant.
6. Return the cooked beef to the pan.
7. Toss in sliced green onions and stir until everything is well-coated.
8. Serve hot over cooked white rice.

Sweet and Sour Pork

 4 servings   35 Mins   Kcal : 380   Fat: 15g carbs : 40g protein : 20g

Sweet and Sour Pork is a classic Chinese dish featuring crispy pieces of pork tossed in a tangy and sweet sauce with colorful bell peppers and pineapple.

INGREDIENTS

- 1 pound pork tenderloin, cut into bite-sized pieces
- 1 cup cornstarch
- Vegetable oil for frying
- 1/2 cup bell peppers (red and green), diced
- 1/2 cup pineapple chunks
- 1/2 cup onion, diced
- 1/2 cup carrot, thinly sliced
- 1/4 cup ketchup
- 2 tablespoons soy sauce
- 2 tablespoons rice vinegar
- 2 tablespoons brown sugar
- 1 tablespoon cornstarch mixed with 2 tablespoons water
- Cooked white rice for serving

INSTRUCTIONS

1. Dredge pork pieces in cornstarch, ensuring each piece is well-coated.
2. Heat vegetable oil in a wok or deep pan over medium-high heat. Fry the pork until golden brown and crispy. Remove and drain on paper towels.
3. In a separate pan, sauté diced bell peppers, pineapple chunks, onion, and sliced carrot.
4. . In a bowl, mix ketchup, soy sauce, rice vinegar, and brown sugar. Pour the sauce over the vegetables.
5. Add the fried pork to the pan.
6. Pour the cornstarch-water mixture over the pork and vegetables. Stir until the sauce thickens.
7. Serve hot over cooked white rice.

Mapo Tofu

 4 servings   30 Mins   Kcal : 280   Fat: 18g   carbs : 15g   protein : 18g

Mapo Tofu is a spicy and flavorful Sichuan dish that features soft tofu cubes in a bold and aromatic sauce made with ground pork, fermented black beans, and Sichuan peppercorns.

INGREDIENTS

- 1 block (14 oz) silken tofu, cut into cubes
- 1/2 pound ground pork
- 2 tablespoons vegetable oil
- 2 tablespoons fermented black beans, rinsed and minced
- 2 tablespoons chili bean paste
- 1 tablespoon soy sauce
- 1 tablespoon Shaoxing wine (or dry sherry)
- 1 teaspoon sugar
- 1 teaspoon Sichuan peppercorns, crushed
- 3 cloves garlic, minced
- 1 tablespoon ginger, grated
- 2 green onions, chopped
- Cooked white rice for serving

INSTRUCTIONS

1. In a wok or skillet, heat vegetable oil over medium heat.
2. Add ground pork and cook until browned.
3. Stir in fermented black beans, chili bean paste, soy sauce, Shaoxing wine, sugar, and crushed Sichuan peppercorns.
4. Add minced garlic and grated ginger, stirring until fragrant.
5. Gently add tofu cubes to the sauce, being careful not to break them.
6. Simmer for a few minutes until the tofu is heated through and coated in the sauce.
7. Garnish with chopped green onions.
8. Serve hot over cooked white rice.

Dim Sum: Shumai (Pork Dumplings)

 4 servings   45 Mins   Kcal : 220   Fat: 10g carbs : 18g protein : 15g

Shumai, also known as pork dumplings, is a classic dim sum dish. These open-faced dumplings are filled with a savory mixture of ground pork, shrimp, and aromatics, creating a delightful bite-sized treat.

INGREDIENTS

- 1/2 pound ground pork
- 1/4 pound shrimp, finely chopped
- 2 tablespoons soy sauce
- 1 tablespoon sesame oil
- 1 tablespoon cornstarch
- 1 tablespoon sugar
- 1 teaspoon ginger, grated
- 1 teaspoon garlic, minced
- Wonton wrappers
- Green peas or carrot slices for garnish (optional)
- Soy sauce and chili oil for dipping

INSTRUCTIONS

1. In a bowl, mix ground pork, chopped shrimp, soy sauce, sesame oil, cornstarch, sugar, grated ginger, and minced garlic.
2. Place a spoonful of the mixture onto each wonton wrapper.
3. Gather the edges of the wrapper and pinch to create a pleated effect, leaving the center exposed.
4. Top each dumpling with a green pea or a thin slice of carrot if desired.
5. Steam the shumai for 10-12 minutes until cooked through.
6. Serve hot with soy sauce and chili oil for dipping.

Peking Duck

 4 servings   24 Hours   Kcal : 350   Fat: 28g carbs : 10g protein : 25g

Peking Duck is a famous Chinese dish with crispy, flavorful duck skin wrapped in thin pancakes with hoisin sauce, cucumber, and green onions. It's a delicious and indulgent treat

INGREDIENTS

- **1 whole duck**
- **1/4 cup soy sauce**
- **1/4 cup hoisin sauce**
- **2 tablespoons honey**
- **1 tablespoon Shaoxing wine (or dry sherry)**
- **1 teaspoon five-spice powder**
- **Thin pancakes (store-bought or homemade)**
- **Cucumber, julienned**
- **Green onions, julienned**

INSTRUCTIONS

1. Clean and dry the duck. Rub the duck with a mixture of soy sauce, hoisin sauce, honey, Shaoxing wine, and five-spice powder.
2. Hang the duck in a cool, dry place for at least 24 hours to air-dry the skin.
3. Preheat the oven and roast the duck until the skin is crispy and the meat is tender.
4. Slice the duck and serve with thin pancakes, hoisin sauce, julienned cucumber, and green onions.
5. Assemble by placing a slice of duck, cucumber, and green onions in a pancake and roll it up.

Chinese Hot and Sour Soup

 4 servings   30 Mins   Kcal : 120   Fat: 6g   carbs : 10g   protein : 8g

Chinese Hot and Sour Soup is a flavorful and comforting soup with a balance of spicy and tangy flavors. It features tofu, mushrooms, bamboo shoots, and a variety of spices.

INGREDIENTS

- 4 cups chicken or vegetable broth
- 1/4 cup soy sauce
- 3 tablespoons rice vinegar
- 1 tablespoon sesame oil
- 1 teaspoon sugar
- 1/2 cup tofu, diced
- 1/2 cup shiitake mushrooms, sliced
- 1/4 cup bamboo shoots, julienned
- 2 tablespoons cornstarch mixed with 3 tablespoons water
- 2 eggs, beaten
- Green onions, chopped, for garnish
- White pepper and chili oil, to taste

INSTRUCTIONS

1. In a pot, bring chicken or vegetable broth to a simmer.
2. Add soy sauce, rice vinegar, sesame oil, and sugar.
3. Stir in diced tofu, sliced shiitake mushrooms, and julienned bamboo shoots.
4. Mix cornstarch with water and add it to the soup to thicken.
5. Slowly pour beaten eggs into the soup, stirring gently to create ribbons.
6. Season with white pepper and chili oil to taste.
7. Garnish with chopped green onions before serving.

Chicken Lo Mein

 4 servings   25 Mins   Kcal : 320   Fat: 8g carbs : 54g protein : 20g

Chicken Lo Mein is a stir-fried noodle dish loaded with tender chicken, colorful vegetables, and flavorful lo mein sauce. It's a quick and satisfying meal.

INGREDIENTS

- 8 oz lo mein noodles
- 1/2 pound boneless, skinless chicken breasts, thinly sliced
- 2 tablespoons soy sauce
- 1 tablespoon oyster sauce
- 1 tablespoon hoisin sauce
- 1 tablespoon sesame oil
- 1 teaspoon sugar
- 2 tablespoons vegetable oil
- 2 cups broccoli florets
- 1 bell pepper, thinly sliced
- 2 carrots, julienned
- 2 cloves garlic, minced
- 2 green onions, sliced

INSTRUCTIONS

1. Cook lo mein noodles according to package instructions. Drain and set aside.
2. In a bowl, marinate sliced chicken in soy sauce, oyster sauce, hoisin sauce, sesame oil, and sugar.
3. Heat vegetable oil in a wok or skillet over high heat. Stir-fry marinated chicken until browned.
4. Add broccoli, bell pepper, carrots, minced garlic, and sliced green onions. Stir-fry until vegetables are crisp-tender.
5. Toss in cooked lo mein noodles, ensuring they are well-coated in the sauce.
6. Serve hot, garnished with extra green onions.

Fried Rice with Vegetables

 4 servings   20 Mins   Kcal : 250 Fat: 10g carbs : 35g protein : 8g

Fried Rice with Vegetables is a versatile and quick Chinese dish that transforms leftover rice into a flavorful and satisfying meal. Packed with colorful vegetables, it's a great way to use up ingredients in your kitchen.

INGREDIENTS

- **3 cups cooked jasmine rice, chilled**
- **2 tablespoons vegetable oil**
- **1 cup mixed vegetables (peas, carrots, corn)**
- **2 eggs, beaten**
- **2 tablespoons soy sauce**
- **1 tablespoon oyster sauce**
- **1 teaspoon sesame oil**
- **2 green onions, chopped**

INSTRUCTIONS

1. Heat vegetable oil in a wok or skillet over medium-high heat.
2. Add mixed vegetables and stir-fry until they are heated through.
3. Push the vegetables to one side of the wok and pour beaten **eggs into the other side. Scramble the eggs until just cooked.**
4. Combine the cooked vegetables with the scrambled eggs.
5. Add chilled cooked rice to the wok, breaking up any clumps.
6. Drizzle soy sauce, oyster sauce, and sesame oil over the rice. Toss everything together to ensure even coating.
7. Stir-fry for a few more minutes until the rice is heated through.
8. Garnish with chopped green onions before serving.

Ma Po Eggplant

 4 servings 30 Mins Kcal : 280   Fat: 18g carbs : 20g protein : 15g

Ma Po Eggplant is a flavorful and spicy Sichuan dish featuring eggplant cooked in a rich and aromatic sauce with ground pork and fermented black beans.

INGREDIENTS

- 2 medium-sized Chinese eggplants, cut into bite-sized pieces
- 1/2 pound ground pork
- 3 tablespoons vegetable oil
- 2 tablespoons doubanjiang (fermented broad bean paste with chili)
- 1 tablespoon soy sauce
- 1 tablespoon Shaoxing wine (or dry sherry)
- 1 tablespoon sugar
- 1 teaspoon Sichuan peppercorns, crushed
- 3 cloves garlic, minced
- 1 tablespoon ginger, grated
- 2 green onions, chopped
- Cooked white rice for serving

INSTRUCTIONS

1. Heat vegetable oil in a wok or skillet over medium heat.
2. Add ground pork and cook until browned.
3. Stir in doubanjiang, soy sauce, Shaoxing wine, sugar, and crushed Sichuan peppercorns.
4. Add minced garlic and grated ginger, stirring until fragrant.
5. Add eggplant pieces to the sauce, tossing to coat evenly.
6. Cover and let it simmer until the eggplant is tender.
7. Garnish with chopped green onions.
8. Serve hot over cooked white rice.

Cantonese-Style Steamed Fish

 2-4 servings 20 Mins Kcal : 180   Fat: 8g carbs : 4g protein : 25g

Cantonese-Style Steamed Fish is a delicate and healthy Chinese dish. The fish is steamed to perfection and topped with a flavorful sauce made with soy sauce, ginger, and green onions.

INGREDIENTS

- **1 whole white-fleshed fish (such as sea bass or snapper), scaled and cleaned**
- **2 tablespoons soy sauce**
- **1 tablespoon oyster sauce**
- **1 tablespoon Shaoxing wine (or dry sherry)**
- **1 tablespoon sesame oil**
- **2 teaspoons sugar**
- **3 slices ginger**
- **2 green onions, sliced**
- **Fresh cilantro for garnish**

INSTRUCTIONS

1. Clean the fish and make three diagonal cuts on each side.
2. Place the fish on a heatproof dish that fits inside your steamer.
3. In a small bowl, mix soy sauce, oyster sauce, Shaoxing wine, sesame oil, and sugar.
4. Pour the sauce over the fish, ensuring it gets into the cuts.
5. Scatter ginger slices over the fish.
6. Steam the fish for about 12-15 minutes or until cooked through.
7. Garnish with sliced green onions and fresh cilantro.
8. Serve hot with steamed rice.

Wonton Soup

 4 servings   30 Mins   Kcal : 220   Fat: 15g carbs : 10g protein : 18g

Wonton Soup is a comforting Chinese soup featuring delicate wontons filled with a mixture of ground pork and shrimp, served in a clear and flavorful broth.

INGREDIENTS

- 1/2 pound ground pork
- 1/4 pound shrimp, finely chopped
- 1 tablespoon soy sauce
- 1 tablespoon sesame oil
- 1 teaspoon sugar
- 1 teaspoon ginger, grated
- 1 teaspoon cornstarch
- Wonton wrappers
- 4 cups chicken broth
- Bok choy or baby spinach, for serving
- Green onions, chopped, for garnish

INSTRUCTIONS

1. In a bowl, mix ground pork, chopped shrimp, soy sauce, sesame oil, sugar, grated ginger, and cornstarch.
2. Place a teaspoon of the filling in the center of each wonton wrapper.
3. Fold the wonton into a triangle, sealing the edges.
4. Bring the two corners of the triangle together, sealing them with a bit of water.
5. In a pot, bring chicken broth to a simmer.
6. Add wontons to the broth and cook until they float to the surface.
7. Add bok choy or baby spinach to the soup and cook until just wilted.
8. Garnish with chopped green onions before serving.

Mongolian Beef

 4 servings   25 Mins   Kcal : 350   Fat: 15g carbs : 30g protein : 25g

Mongolian Beef is a savory and slightly sweet Chinese stir-fry dish featuring tender slices of beef in a rich sauce made with soy sauce, hoisin sauce, and brown sugar.

INGREDIENTS

- **1 pound flank steak, thinly sliced**
- **1/4 cup cornstarch**
- **2 tablespoons vegetable oil**
- **3 cloves garlic, minced**
- **1 tablespoon ginger, grated**
- **1/2 cup soy sauce**
- **1/4 cup hoisin sauce**
- **1/4 cup brown sugar**
- **2 tablespoons water**
- **Green onions, sliced, for garnish**
- **Sesame seeds, for garnish**
- **Cooked white rice for serving**

INSTRUCTIONS

1. Toss sliced flank steak in cornstarch, ensuring each piece is well-coated.
2. Heat vegetable oil in a wok or skillet over high heat.
3. Stir-fry beef until browned and crispy. Remove and set aside.
4. In the same pan, add minced garlic and grated ginger. Stir until fragrant.
5. Mix soy sauce, hoisin sauce, brown sugar, and water. Pour the sauce over the garlic and ginger.
6. Return the cooked beef to the pan, tossing to coat in the sauce.
7. Garnish with sliced green onions and sesame seeds.
8. Serve hot over cooked white rice.

Chinese BBQ Pork (Char Siu)

 4 servings   2 Hrs marinating + 30 Mins cooking   Kcal : 280   Fat: 18g carbs : 10g protein : 20g

Chinese BBQ Pork, known as Char Siu, is a popular Cantonese dish featuring sweet and savory roasted pork with a glossy, flavorful glaze. It's often used in various Chinese dishes and makes a delicious standalone dish.

INGREDIENTS

- 1 pound pork shoulder or pork belly, thinly sliced
- 2 tablespoons soy sauce
- 2 tablespoons hoisin sauce
- 2 tablespoons oyster sauce
- 2 tablespoons sugar
- 1 tablespoon Shaoxing wine (or dry sherry)
- 1 teaspoon five-spice powder
- 2 cloves garlic, minced
- Red food coloring (optional, for traditional color)
- Bamboo skewers, soaked in water
- Honey for glazing

INSTRUCTIONS

1. In a bowl, mix soy sauce, hoisin sauce, oyster sauce, sugar, Shaoxing wine, five-spice powder, minced garlic, and red food coloring (if using).
2. Marinate sliced pork in the sauce for at least 2 hours or overnight.
3. Preheat the oven or grill.
4. Thread marinated pork slices onto bamboo skewers.
5. Roast or grill the pork, basting with honey for a glossy finish, until cooked through.
6. Serve hot, sliced into bite-sized pieces.

Kung Pao Chicken

 4 servings   30 Mins   Kcal : 300 Fat: 15g carbs : 20g protein : 25g

Kung Pao Chicken is a classic Sichuan dish known for its bold flavors, combining tender chicken, peanuts, and vegetables in a spicy and tangy sauce.

INGREDIENTS

- 1 pound boneless, skinless chicken breasts, diced
- 1/2 cup peanuts, roasted
- 2 tablespoons vegetable oil
- 2 tablespoons soy sauce
- 1 tablespoon rice vinegar
- 1 tablespoon hoisin sauce
- 1 tablespoon sugar
- 1 teaspoon cornstarch
- 2 teaspoons Sichuan peppercorns, crushed
- 3 dried red chilies, chopped
- 3 cloves garlic, minced
- 1 tablespoon ginger, grated
- 3 green onions, sliced
- Cooked white rice for serving

INSTRUCTIONS

1. In a bowl, mix diced chicken with soy sauce, rice vinegar, hoisin sauce, sugar, and cornstarch.
2. Heat vegetable oil in a wok or skillet over high heat.
3. Stir-fry marinated chicken until browned and cooked through. Remove and set aside.
4. In the same pan, add crushed Sichuan peppercorns, dried red chilies, minced garlic, and grated ginger. Stir until fragrant.
5. Add roasted peanuts and sliced green onions, tossing to combine.
6. Return the cooked chicken to the pan, coating it in the spicy sauce.
7. Serve hot over cooked white rice.

Chinese Vegetable Stir-Fry

 4 servings   20 Mins   Kcal : 150   Fat:8g carbs : 28g protein : 5g

Chinese Vegetable Stir-Fry is a quick and healthy dish featuring a medley of colorful vegetables stir-fried to perfection. It's versatile, allowing you to use your favorite vegetables.

INGREDIENTS

- 2 cups broccoli florets
- 1 bell pepper, sliced
- 1 carrot, julienned
- 1 cup snap peas, trimmed
- 1/2 cup baby corn
- 2 tablespoons vegetable oil
- 2 tablespoons soy sauce
- 1 tablespoon oyster sauce
- 1 teaspoon sugar
- 1 teaspoon sesame oil
- 2 cloves garlic, minced
- 1 tablespoon ginger, grated
- Cooked jasmine rice for serving

INSTRUCTIONS

1. In a wok or skillet, heat vegetable oil over high heat.
2. Add broccoli, bell pepper, julienned carrot, snap peas, and baby corn. Stir-fry until vegetables are crisp-tender.
3. In a small bowl, mix soy sauce, oyster sauce, sugar, and sesame oil.
4. Push the vegetables to the side of the wok and add minced garlic and grated ginger. Stir until fragrant.
5. Pour the sauce over the vegetables, tossing to coat evenly.
6. Serve the stir-fried vegetables over cooked jasmine rice.

Chinese Egg Fried Rice

 4 servings   20 Mins   Kcal : 250   Fat: 10g carbs : 35g protein : 8g

Chinese Egg Fried Rice is a classic and simple dish that transforms leftover rice into a delicious and satisfying meal. It's quick to make and versatile, allowing you to add your favorite ingredients.

INGREDIENTS

- **3 cups cooked jasmine rice, chilled**
- **2 tablespoons vegetable oil**
- **2 eggs, beaten**
- **1 cup mixed vegetables (peas, carrots, corn)**
- **2 tablespoons soy sauce**
- **1 tablespoon oyster sauce**
- **1 teaspoon sesame oil**
- **2 green onions, chopped**

INSTRUCTIONS

1. Heat vegetable oil in a wok or skillet over medium-high heat.
2. Pour beaten eggs into the pan, stirring until just cooked.
3. Add mixed vegetables and stir-fry until they are heated through.
4. Push the eggs and vegetables to one side of the wok. Add chilled cooked rice to the other side, breaking up any clumps.
5. Drizzle soy sauce, oyster sauce, and sesame oil over the rice. Toss everything together to ensure even coating.
6. Stir-fry for a few more minutes until the rice is heated through.
7. Garnish with chopped green onions before serving.

Sichuan Dan Dan Noodles

 4 servings   25 Mins   Kcal : 350   Fat: 18g carbs : 30g protein : 15g

Sichuan Dan Dan Noodles are a flavorful and spicy noodle dish featuring ground meat, chili oil, and a nutty sesame sauce. It's a popular street food dish in Sichuan province.

INGREDIENTS

- 8 oz Chinese wheat noodles (or any noodles of your choice)
- 1/2 pound ground pork or chicken
- 2 tablespoons vegetable oil
- 2 tablespoons soy sauce
- 1 tablespoon dark soy sauce
- 1 tablespoon hoisin sauce
- 1 tablespoon rice vinegar
- 1 tablespoon
- sugar
- 1 teaspoon sesame oil
- 2 cloves garlic, minced
- 1 tablespoon ginger, grated
- 2 tablespoons Sichuan chili oil
- Chopped green onions and crushed peanuts for garnish

INSTRUCTIONS

1. Cook noodles according to package instructions. Drain and set aside.
2. In a skillet, heat vegetable oil over medium heat. Add ground pork or chicken, breaking it up as it cooks.
3. Stir in soy sauce, dark soy sauce, hoisin sauce, rice vinegar, sugar, and sesame oil.
4. Add minced garlic and grated ginger, cooking until fragrant.
5. Toss cooked noodles in the skillet with the meat and sauce.
6. Drizzle Sichuan chili oil over the noodles, tossing to combine.
7. Serve hot, garnished with chopped green onions and crushed peanuts.

Dim Sum Shrimp Dumplings (Har Gow)

 4 servings   45 Mins   Kcal : 180   Fat: 8g carbs : 12g protein :15g

Har Gow, or shrimp dumplings, are a classic Cantonese dim sum dish. These delicate dumplings feature a translucent wrapper filled with a flavorful mixture of shrimp and bamboo shoots.

INGREDIENTS

- **1 cup shrimp, peeled and deveined**
- **1/2 cup bamboo shoots, finely chopped**
- **2 tablespoons cornstarch**
- **1 tablespoon soy sauce**
- **1 tablespoon oyster sauce**
- **1 tablespoon sesame oil**
- **1 teaspoon sugar**
- **1/2 teaspoon white pepper**
- **Wonton wrappers**
- **Chives or green onions for garnish**
- **Soy sauce or chili sauce for dipping**

INSTRUCTIONS

1. In a food processor, pulse shrimp until finely chopped.
2. Mix chopped shrimp with bamboo shoots, cornstarch, soy sauce, oyster sauce, sesame oil, sugar, and white pepper.
3. Place a teaspoon of the shrimp mixture in the center of each wonton wrapper.
4. Fold the wrapper in half, sealing the edges with a bit of water.
5. Pleat the edges to create a crescent shape.
6. Steam dumplings for about 8-10 minutes until the wrapper becomes translucent.
7. Garnish with chopped chives or green onions.
8. Serve hot with soy sauce or chili sauce for dipping.

Crispy Spring Rolls

 4 servings   45 Mins   Kcal : 200   Fat: 10g   carbs : 20g   protein : 8g

Crispy Spring Rolls are a popular appetizer in Chinese cuisine. These rolls are filled with a mixture of vegetables, vermicelli noodles, and often include shrimp or ground pork.

INGREDIENTS

- Spring roll wrappers
- 1 cup shredded cabbage
- 1 cup shredded carrots
- 1/2 cup bean sprouts
- 1/2 cup cooked vermicelli noodles
- 1/2 cup shrimp, cooked and chopped (optional)
- 2 tablespoons soy sauce
- 1 tablespoon oyster sauce
- 1 teaspoon sesame oil
- 1 teaspoon sugar
- Vegetable oil for frying
- Sweet chili sauce for dipping

INSTRUCTIONS

1. In a wok or skillet, stir-fry shredded cabbage, carrots, bean sprouts, and cooked vermicelli noodles.
2. Add soy sauce, oyster sauce, sesame oil, and sugar. Toss until well-coated.
3. Place a spoonful of the vegetable mixture onto a spring roll wrapper.
4. Fold the sides of the wrapper over the filling and roll tightly.
5. Seal the edge with a bit of water.
6. Heat vegetable oil in a deep fryer or large skillet.
7. Fry the spring rolls until golden and crispy.
8. Drain on paper towels and serve hot with sweet chili sauce for dipping.

Sweet and Sour Chicken

 4 servings   40 Mins   Kcal : 350   Fat: 15g   carbs : 30g   protein : 20g

Sweet and Sour Chicken is a classic Chinese-American dish featuring crispy chicken coated in a vibrant sweet and tangy sauce with bell peppers and pineapple.

INGREDIENTS

- **1 pound boneless, skinless chicken thighs, cut into bite-sized pieces**
- **1/2 cup cornstarch**
- **Vegetable oil for frying**
- **1 bell pepper, diced**
- **1 cup pineapple chunks**
- **1/2 cup ketchup**
- **1/4 cup rice vinegar**
- **2 tablespoons soy sauce**
- **1/4 cup sugar**
- **1 teaspoon ginger, grated**
- **1 teaspoon garlic, minced**
- **Cooked white rice for serving**

INSTRUCTIONS

1. Coat chicken pieces in cornstarch, shaking off excess.
2. Heat vegetable oil in a wok or deep fryer. Fry the coated chicken until golden and crispy. Remove and drain on paper towels.
3. In a pan, combine ketchup, rice vinegar, soy sauce, sugar, grated ginger, and minced garlic.
4. Heat the sauce until it thickens.
5. Add diced bell pepper and pineapple chunks, tossing to coat in the sauce.
6. Add the fried chicken to the pan, coating it in the sweet and sour sauce.
7. Serve hot over cooked white rice.

Chinese BBQ Buns (Char Siu Bao)

 4 servings   2 Hours   Kcal : 250 Fat:8g carbs : 35g protein : 10g

Char Siu Bao is a popular Cantonese dish that has gained global recognition for its unique combination of textures and flavors. These steamed buns are characterized by their soft, pillowy exterior, which encases a succulent and sweet-savory filling made with char siu, or Chinese BBQ pork.

INGREDIENTS

- 2 cups all-purpose flour
- 1 tablespoon sugar
- 1 teaspoon baking powder
- 1 teaspoon active dry yeast
- 1/2 cup warm water
- 1 tablespoon vegetable oil
- 1 cup char siu (Chinese BBQ pork), diced
- 2 tablespoons soy sauce
- 1 tablespoon oyster sauce
- 1 tablespoon hoisin sauce
- 1 tablespoon sugar
- 1 teaspoon sesame oil

INSTRUCTIONS

1. In a bowl, combine flour, sugar, and baking powder.
2. In a separate bowl, dissolve yeast in warm water. Add it to the dry ingredients.
3. Knead the dough until smooth, then let it rise in a warm place for about 1 hour.
4. While the dough is rising, mix diced char siu with soy sauce, oyster sauce, hoisin sauce, sugar, and sesame oil.
5. Divide the risen dough into small balls. Roll each ball into a thin circle.
6. Place a spoonful of the char siu mixture in the center of each circle. Fold and pinch the edges to seal.
7. Steam the buns for about 15-20 minutes until they are cooked through.
8. Serve the Char Siu Bao warm.

Chinese Almond Cookies

 4 servings   30 Mins   Kcal : 120   Fat: 7g carbs : 12g protein : 2g

Chinese Almond Cookies are crisp and nutty treats often enjoyed during celebrations. They are simple to make and perfect for satisfying a sweet tooth.

INGREDIENTS

- **1 cup butter, softened**
- **1 cup sugar**
- **1 egg**
- **1 teaspoon almond extract**
- **2 1/2 cups all-purpose flour**
- **1/2 cup ground almonds**
- **1/2 teaspoon baking soda**
- **Whole almonds for topping**

INSTRUCTIONS

1. Preheat the oven to 350°F (175°C).
2. In a bowl, cream together softened butter and sugar.
3. Beat in the egg and almond extract.
4. In a separate bowl, whisk together flour, ground almonds, and baking soda.
5. Gradually add the dry ingredients to the wet ingredients, mixing until combined.
6. Roll the cookie dough into small balls and place them on a baking sheet.
7. Flatten each ball slightly and press a whole almond into the center.
8. Bake for about 12-15 minutes or until the edges are golden.
9. Allow the cookies to cool before serving.

Japanese Cuisine

Sushi Rolls (Maki)

 4 servings   30 Mins   Kcal : Varies   Fat: Varies carbs : Varies protein : Varies

Sushi Rolls, or Maki, are a staple in Japanese cuisine. These rolls typically include ingredients like fresh fish, vegetables, and seaweed, wrapped around seasoned rice.

INGREDIENTS

- **Nori (seaweed) sheets**
- **Sushi rice (vinegared rice)**
- **Fresh fish (e.g., tuna, salmon)**
- **Vegetables (e.g., cucumber, avocado)**
- **Soy sauce, for dipping**
- **Pickled ginger and wasabi, for serving**

INSTRUCTIONS

1. Place a sheet of nori on a bamboo sushi rolling mat.
2. Wet your hands to prevent sticking, then spread a thin layer of sushi rice over the nori.
3. Arrange thin strips of fresh fish and vegetables along the center of the rice.
4. Roll the sushi tightly using the bamboo mat.
5. Seal the edge of the nori with a little water.
6. Slice the roll into bite-sized pieces.
7. Serve with soy sauce, pickled ginger, and wasabi.

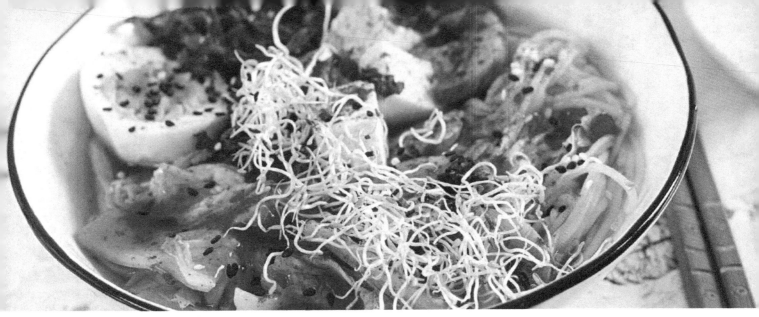

Ramen Noodles with Miso Broth

 4 servings   20 Mins   Kcal : 300   Fat: 8g carbs : 45g protein : 10g

Ramen Noodles with Miso Broth is a comforting Japanese dish featuring chewy noodles in a flavorful miso-based soup with vegetables and protein.

INGREDIENTS

- Ramen noodles
- 4 cups vegetable or chicken broth
- 3 tablespoons white miso paste
- 1 tablespoon soy sauce
- 1 tablespoon sesame oil
- 1 tablespoon mirin
- 1 cup sliced shiitake mushrooms
- 1 cup baby spinach
- Green onions and nori for garnish

INSTRUCTIONS

1. Cook ramen noodles according to package instructions.
2. In a pot, heat broth and whisk in miso paste until dissolved.
3. Add soy sauce, sesame oil, mirin, and sliced shiitake mushrooms. Simmer until mushrooms are tender.
4. Add cooked ramen noodles and baby spinach, cooking until spinach wilts.
5. Serve hot, garnished with sliced green onions and nori.

Chicken Teriyaki

 4 servings   30 Mins   Kcal : 250   Fat: 10g carbs : 15g protein : 20g

Chicken Teriyaki is a classic Japanese dish featuring tender chicken glazed in a sweet and savory teriyaki sauce.

INGREDIENTS

- **1 pound boneless, skinless chicken thighs, sliced**
- **1/2 cup soy sauce**
- **1/4 cup mirin**
- **1/4 cup sake**
- **3 tablespoons sugar**
- **1 tablespoon vegetable oil**
- **Sesame seeds and sliced green onions for garnish**

INSTRUCTIONS

1. In a bowl, mix soy sauce, mirin, sake, and sugar to create the teriyaki sauce.
2. Heat vegetable oil in a skillet over medium-high heat.
3. Cook sliced chicken until browned and cooked through.
4. Pour teriyaki sauce over the chicken, simmering until the sauce thickens.
5. Garnish with sesame seeds and sliced green onions.
6. Serve hot over rice.

Tempura Shrimp and Vegetables

 4 servings   20 Mins   Kcal : Varies   Fat: Varies   carbs : Varies   protein : Varies

Tempura is a Japanese dish featuring lightly battered and fried seafood and vegetables. It's known for its crispy texture and light, flavorful taste.

INGREDIENTS

- **Shrimp, peeled and deveined**
- **Assorted vegetables (e.g., sweet potato, zucchini, bell pepper)**
- **Tempura batter mix**
- **Ice-cold water**
- **Vegetable oil for frying**
- **Tempura dipping sauce**

INSTRUCTIONS

1. Prepare tempura batter according to package instructions, using ice-cold water.
2. Dip shrimp and vegetables into the batter, coating them evenly.
3. Heat vegetable oil in a deep fryer or large pot.
4. Fry the battered shrimp and vegetables until golden brown and crispy.
5. Drain on paper towels.
6. Serve hot with tempura dipping sauce.

Chawanmushi (Savory Egg Custard)

 4 servings   30 Mins   Kcal : 150 Fat: 8g carbs : 6g protein : 12g

Chawanmushi is a delicate Japanese dish featuring a savory egg custard with ingredients like chicken, shrimp, and vegetables.

INGREDIENTS

- **4 large eggs**
- **2 cups dashi (Japanese broth)**
- **1 tablespoon soy sauce**
- **1 tablespoon mirin**
- **1/2 teaspoon salt**
- **Chicken pieces, shrimp, mushrooms, and ginkgo nuts (optional)**
- **Chopped green onions for garnish**

INSTRUCTIONS

1. In a bowl, whisk eggs and gradually add dashi, soy sauce, mirin, and salt.
2. Strain the egg mixture to ensure a smooth custard.
3. Divide chicken, shrimp, mushrooms, and ginkgo nuts among serving cups.
4. Pour the egg mixture over the ingredients in each cup.
5. Steam the custards for about 15-20 minutes until set.
6. Garnish with chopped green onions.
7. Serve hot.

Okonomiyaki (Japanese Savory Pancake)

 4 servings   30 Mins   Kcal : 250   Fat: 10g carbs : 30g protein : 10g

Okonomiyaki is a savory Japanese pancake filled with shredded cabbage, meat (usually pork or seafood), and topped with a sweet and tangy okonomiyaki sauce.

INGREDIENTS

- **2 cups shredded cabbage**
- **1 cup all-purpose flour**
- **1/2 cup dashi (Japanese broth)**
- **2 eggs**
- **1/2 cup sliced green onions**
- **1/2 cup cooked and diced meat or seafood (e.g., pork, shrimp)**
- **Okonomiyaki sauce**
- **Kewpie mayonnaise**
- **Bonito flakes and nori strips for garnish**

INSTRUCTIONS

1. In a bowl, combine shredded cabbage, all-purpose flour, dashi, eggs, sliced green onions, and diced meat or seafood.
2. Heat a griddle or non-stick skillet over medium heat.
3. Spoon the batter onto the griddle to form pancakes.
4. Cook until the bottom is golden brown, then flip and cook the other side.
5. Drizzle okonomiyaki sauce and kewpie mayonnaise over the pancakes.
6. Sprinkle with bonito flakes and garnish with nori strips.
7. Serve hot.

Yakitori (Grilled Chicken Skewers)

 4 servings   30 Mins   Kcal : 200   Fat: 10g carbs : 10g protein : 15g

Yakitori is a popular Japanese dish consisting of grilled chicken skewers, typically flavored with a sweet and savory soy-based glaze.

INGREDIENTS

- **1 pound chicken thighs, cut into bite-sized pieces**
- **Soy sauce**
- **Mirin (sweet rice wine)**
- **Sake**
- **Sugar**
- **Bamboo skewers, soaked in water**
- **Green onions, for garnish**

INSTRUCTIONS

1. Thread chicken pieces onto the soaked bamboo skewers.
2. In a saucepan, mix equal parts soy sauce, mirin, sake, and a tablespoon of sugar.
3. Heat the sauce over medium heat until it thickens slightly.
4. Grill the chicken skewers, basting with the sauce until fully cooked.
5. Garnish with chopped green onions.
6. Serve hot.

Miso Soup with Tofu and Wakame

 4 servings   15 Mins   Kcal : 180   Fat: 3g   carbs : 8g protein : 5g

Miso Soup is a comforting Japanese soup made with miso paste, tofu, seaweed (wakame), and other ingredients. It's a staple in Japanese cuisine.

INGREDIENTS

- **4 cups dashi (Japanese broth)**
- **3 tablespoons miso paste**
- **1/2 cup tofu, cubed**
- **2 tablespoons dried wakame seaweed, rehydrated**
- **Green onions, sliced, for garnish**

INSTRUCTIONS

1. In a pot, heat dashi until almost boiling.
2. Dissolve miso paste in a small amount of dashi and add it to the pot.
3. Add cubed tofu and rehydrated wakame seaweed.
4. Simmer for a few minutes without boiling.
5. Garnish with sliced green onions.
6. Serve hot.

Donburi (Rice Bowl with Toppings)

 4 servings 20 Mins Kcal : 350 Fat: 15g carbs : 30g protein : 25g

Donburi is a Japanese dish consisting of a bowl of rice topped with various ingredients. One popular variation is Gyudon, featuring thinly sliced beef and onions.

INGREDIENTS

- **1 pound thinly sliced beef (e.g., sirloin or ribeye)**
- **1 onion, thinly sliced**
- **2 tablespoons soy sauce**
- **2 tablespoons mirin**
- **1 tablespoon sugar**
- **1 tablespoon sake**
- **Cooked rice**
- **Green onions, sliced, for garnish**
- **Pickled ginger, for serving**

INSTRUCTIONS

1. In a skillet, cook thinly sliced beef until browned.
2. Add sliced onions and cook until softened.
3. In a bowl, mix soy sauce, mirin, sugar, and sake.
4. Pour the sauce over the beef and onions, simmering until the sauce thickens.
5. Serve the beef and onions over a bowl of cooked rice.
6. Garnish with sliced green onions.
7. Serve hot with pickled ginger on the side.

Sunomono (Japanese Cucumber Salad)

 4 servings   15 Mins   Kcal : 40   Fat: 0g carbs : 10g protein : 1g

Sunomono is a refreshing Japanese cucumber salad with a sweet and tangy vinegar dressing. It's a perfect side dish or appetizer.

INGREDIENTS

- **2 cucumbers, thinly sliced**
- **1/4 cup rice vinegar**
- **2 tablespoons sugar**
- **1 teaspoon soy sauce**
- **Sesame seeds, for garnish**
- **Chopped fresh cilantro or mint, for garnish**

INSTRUCTIONS

1. Thinly slice cucumbers and place them in a bowl.
2. In a small saucepan, heat rice vinegar, sugar, and soy sauce until sugar dissolves.
3. Pour the dressing over the sliced cucumbers and toss to coat.
4. Chill the salad in the refrigerator for at least 30 minutes.
5. Garnish with sesame seeds and chopped cilantro or mint.
6. Serve cold.

Ebi Nigiri (Shrimp Nigiri Sushi)

 4 servings 20 Mins Kcal : Varies Fat: Varies carbs : Varies protein : Varies

Ebi Nigiri is a type of nigiri sushi featuring a perfectly seasoned sushi rice base topped with a piece of fresh shrimp.

INGREDIENTS

- **Sushi rice**
- **Fresh shrimp, deveined and cooked**
- **Soy sauce**
- **Wasabi**
- **Pickled ginger**

INSTRUCTIONS

1. Prepare sushi rice and let it cool to room temperature.
2. Take a small amount of rice and shape it into an oblong mound.
3. Place a piece of cooked shrimp on top of the rice.
4. Optionally, brush a small amount of soy sauce on top of the shrimp.
5. Serve the Ebi Nigiri with wasabi and pickled ginger on the side.
6. Repeat to make additional nigiri.

Tonkatsu (Breaded and Fried Pork Cutlet)

 4 servings   30 Mins   Kcal : 400 Fat: 20g carbs : 30g protein : 25g

Tonkatsu is a Japanese dish that features a breaded and deep-fried pork cutlet. It's typically served with shredded cabbage and tonkatsu sauce.

INGREDIENTS

- **4 pork loin cutlets**
- **Salt and pepper**
- **Flour, for dredging**
- **2 eggs, beaten**
- **Panko breadcrumbs**
- **Vegetable oil, for frying**
- **Shredded cabbage, for serving**
- **Tonkatsu sauce**

INSTRUCTIONS

1. Season pork cutlets with salt and pepper.
2. Dredge each cutlet in flour, dip in beaten eggs, and coat with panko breadcrumbs.
3. Heat vegetable oil in a pan and fry cutlets until golden brown and cooked through.
4. Drain on paper towels.
5. Slice the tonkatsu into strips.
6. Serve over a bed of shredded cabbage.
7. Drizzle tonkatsu sauce over the top.

Gyoza (Japanese Dumplings)

 4 servings   45 Mins   Kcal : 200   Fat: 10g carbs : 15g protein : 10g

Gyoza are Japanese dumplings filled with a mixture of ground meat and vegetables, wrapped in a thin dough and pan-fried to perfection.

INGREDIENTS

- Gyoza wrappers
- 1/2 pound ground pork
- 1 cup finely shredded cabbage
- 2 cloves garlic, minced
- 1 tablespoon ginger, grated
- 2 tablespoons soy sauce
- 1 tablespoon sesame oil
- 1 teaspoon sugar
- Vegetable oil, for pan-frying
- Dipping sauce (soy sauce, rice vinegar, and chili oil)

INSTRUCTIONS

1. In a bowl, mix ground pork, shredded cabbage, minced garlic, grated ginger, soy sauce, sesame oil, and sugar.
2. Place a spoonful of the filling in the center of a gyoza wrapper.
3. Moisten the edge of the wrapper with water and fold in half, pleating the edges to seal.
4. Heat vegetable oil in a pan and arrange gyoza in a single layer.
5. Fry until the bottoms are golden brown.
6. Add water to the pan and cover to steam the gyoza until cooked through.
7. Serve with dipping sauce.

Matcha Green Tea Ice Cream

 6 servings   4 Hours   Kcal : 300   Fat: 20g carbs : 25g protein : 5g

Matcha Green Tea Ice Cream is a popular Japanese dessert with a rich and earthy flavor. It's made with matcha powder, giving it a vibrant green color.

INGREDIENTS

- **2 cups heavy cream**
- **1 cup whole milk**
- **3/4 cup sugar**
- **2 tablespoons matcha powder**
- **6 egg yolks**

INSTRUCTIONS

1. In a saucepan, heat heavy cream, whole milk, and sugar until it begins to simmer.
2. In a bowl, whisk matcha powder with a small amount of hot milk mixture to create a paste.
3. Whisk the matcha paste into the hot milk mixture.
4. In a separate bowl, whisk egg yolks.
5. Slowly pour the hot milk mixture into the egg yolks, whisking continuously.
6. Return the mixture to the saucepan and heat until it thickens, stirring constantly.
7. Strain the mixture and let it cool.
8. Churn the mixture in an ice cream maker according to the manufacturer's instructions.
9. Freeze the ice cream until firm.
10. Serve the Matcha Green Tea Ice Cream and enjoy!

Nikujaga (Japanese Meat and Potato Stew)

 4 servings   45 Mins   Kcal : 300   Fat: 10g   carbs : 40g   protein : 15g

Nikujaga is a hearty Japanese stew featuring tender meat, potatoes, and vegetables simmered in a sweet and savory soy-based broth.

INGREDIENTS

- 1/2 lb thinly sliced beef
- 4 potatoes, peeled and sliced
- 2 carrots, sliced
- 1 onion, thinly sliced
- 1 cup green beans, cut into bite-sized pieces
- 1 cup dashi (Japanese stock)
- 1/4 cup soy sauce
- 2 tablespoons mirin
- 2 tablespoons sugar

INSTRUCTIONS

1. In a pot, layer potatoes, carrots, onions, and beef.
2. Mix dashi, soy sauce, mirin, and sugar; pour over the ingredients.
3. Simmer until potatoes are tender.

Chirashizushi (Scattered Sushi Bowl)

 4 servings   30 Mins   Kcal : 350   Fat: 10g carbs : 50g protein : 15g

Chirashizushi is a colorful and vibrant dish featuring sushi rice topped with an assortment of fresh sashimi, vegetables, and pickles.

INGREDIENTS

- **2 cups sushi rice**
- **Assorted sashimi (tuna, salmon, shrimp)**
- **Vegetables (cucumber, radish, avocado)**
- **Pickled ginger, wasabi, soy sauce for serving**
- **Sesame seeds for garnish**

INSTRUCTIONS

1. Spread sushi rice in a bowl.
2. Arrange sashimi and vegetables on top.
3. Garnish with pickled ginger, wasabi, and sesame seeds.

Katsudon (Pork Cutlet Bowl)

 4 servings   40 Mins   Kcal : 450   Fat: 15g carbs : 60g protein : 20g

Katsudon is a comforting Japanese rice bowl topped with a crispy pork cutlet, onions, and a savory sweet sauce.

INGREDIENTS

- **4 pork loin cutlets**
- **1 cup all-purpose flour**
- **2 eggs, beaten**
- **Panko breadcrumbs**
- **1 onion, thinly sliced**
- **1/4 cup soy sauce**
- **2 tablespoons mirin**
- **2 tablespoons sugar**
- **2 cups cooked rice**

INSTRUCTIONS

1. Dredge pork in flour, dip in eggs, coat with breadcrumbs, and fry.
2. In a pan, sauté sliced onions; add soy sauce, mirin, and sugar.
3. Place fried pork on rice; pour onion mixture over.

Soba Noodle Salad with Sesame Dressing

 4 servings   20 Mins   Kcal : 250   Fat: 5g carbs : 45g protein : 8g

Soba Noodle Salad is a refreshing Japanese dish featuring cold buckwheat noodles, crisp vegetables, and a flavorful sesame dressing.

INGREDIENTS

- 8 oz soba noodles
- 1 cup julienned carrots
- 1 cup sliced cucumber
- 1/4 cup soy sauce
- 2 tablespoons rice vinegar
- 1 tablespoon sesame oil
- 1 tablespoon sugar
- Sesame seeds for garnish

INSTRUCTIONS

1. Cook soba noodles; cool under running water.
2. Toss noodles with carrots and cucumber.
3. Mix soy sauce, rice vinegar, sesame oil, and sugar; dress noodles.
4. Garnish with sesame seeds.

Tamago Sushi (Sweet Japanese Omelette Sushi)

 4 servings   20 Mins   Kcal : 180   Fat: 8g carbs : 15g protein : 8g

Tamago Sushi features a sweet and fluffy Japanese omelette rolled in sushi rice and nori, creating a delightful sushi variation.

INGREDIENTS

- **4 large eggs**
- **2 tablespoons sugar**
- **1 tablespoon soy sauce**
- **1 tablespoon mirin**
- **Sushi rice, nori sheets, and soy sauce for serving**

INSTRUCTIONS

1. Whisk eggs, sugar, soy sauce, and mirin.
2. Cook thin omelette layers; roll and slice into sushi.

Edamame Salad

 4 servings   15 Mins   Kcal : 150   Fat: 8g   carbs : 15g protein : 10g

Edamame Salad is a light and nutritious dish featuring boiled edamame beans, fresh vegetables, and a zesty vinaigrette.

INGREDIENTS

- **2 cups edamame, boiled**
- **1 cup cherry tomatoes, halved**
- **1/2 cup red bell pepper, diced**
- **1/4 cup red onion, finely chopped**
- **2 tablespoons rice vinegar**
- **1 tablespoon soy sauce**
- **1 tablespoon sesame oil**
- **Fresh cilantro for garnish**

INSTRUCTIONS

1. Combine edamame, cherry tomatoes, bell pepper, and red onion.
2. Whisk together rice vinegar, soy sauce, and sesame oil.
3. Toss the salad with the vinaigrette; garnish with cilantro.

Zaru Soba (Cold Soba Noodles)

 4 servings   20 Mins   Kcal : 200   Fat: 2g carbs : 40g protein : 8g

Zaru Soba is a simple and refreshing Japanese dish featuring cold buckwheat noodles served with a soy-based dipping sauce.

INGREDIENTS

- 8 oz soba noodles
- 1/4 cup soy sauce
- 2 tablespoons mirin
- 1 tablespoon rice vinegar
- Green onions and wasabi for serving

INSTRUCTIONS

1. Cook soba noodles; rinse under cold water.
2. Mix soy sauce, mirin, and rice vinegar for dipping.
3. Serve noodles on a bamboo mat with dipping sauce.

Tonjiru (Pork Miso Soup)

 4 servings   40 Mins   Kcal : 250   Fat: 15g carbs : 20g protein :15g

Tonjiru is a hearty Japanese miso soup featuring pork, vegetables, and tofu for a satisfying and comforting meal.

INGREDIENTS

- 1/2 lb pork belly, thinly sliced
- 4 cups dashi (Japanese stock)
- 3 tablespoons miso paste
- 1 onion, sliced
- 2 carrots, sliced
- 1/2 daikon radish, sliced
- 1 cup napa cabbage, chopped
- 1/2 cup tofu, cubed
- Green onions for garnish

INSTRUCTIONS

1. Sauté pork until browned; add dashi, miso, onions, carrots, and daikon.
2. Simmer until vegetables are tender; add tofu and cabbage.
3. Garnish with green onions.

Hōtō (Japanese Pumpkin Noodle Soup)

 4 servings   30 Mins   Kcal : 220   Fat: 5g carbs : 40g protein : 8g

Hōtō is a Japanese noodle soup featuring wide wheat noodles, pumpkin, and a rich miso-based broth.

INGREDIENTS

- **8 oz hōtō noodles**
- **1 cup kabocha pumpkin, diced**
- **4 cups vegetable broth**
- **3 tablespoons miso paste**
- **1 onion, sliced**
- **2 carrots, sliced**
- **2 shiitake mushrooms, sliced**
- **Spinach leaves for garnish**

INSTRUCTIONS

1. Cook hōtō noodles; set aside.
2. In a pot, combine pumpkin, broth, miso, onions, carrots, and shiitake.
3. Simmer until vegetables are tender; add cooked noodles.
4. Garnish with spinach leaves.

Yudofu (Tofu Hot Pot)

 4 servings   20 Mins   Kcal : 100   Fat: 5g carbs : 6g protein : 8g

Yudofu is a simple and soothing Japanese hot pot featuring tofu simmered in a kombu (seaweed) broth.

INGREDIENTS

- 1 block (14 oz) silken tofu, cut into cubes
- 4 cups kombu dashi (seaweed stock)
- 1/4 cup soy sauce
- 2 tablespoons mirin
- Green onions and grated daikon for serving

INSTRUCTIONS

1. Bring kombu dashi to a simmer; add soy sauce and mirin.
2. Add tofu cubes; simmer until heated.
3. Serve with green onions andgrated daikon on the side.

Kenchinjiru (Root Vegetable Soup)

 4 servings   35 Mins   Kcal : 120   Fat: 5g carbs : 15g protein : 8g

Kenchinjiru is a Japanese soup featuring root vegetables, tofu, and shiitake mushrooms in a soy-based broth.

INGREDIENTS

- **4 cups vegetable broth**
- **1 carrot, sliced**
- **1 burdock root, julienned**
- **1 potato, diced**
- **1/2 block firm tofu, cubed**
- **4 shiitake mushrooms, sliced**
- **1 cup spinach leaves**
- **2 tablespoons soy sauce**
- **1 tablespoon mirin**

INSTRUCTIONS

1. Bring vegetable broth to a boil; add carrots, burdock, and potatoes.
2. Add tofu, shiitake mushrooms, and spinach.
3. Season with soy sauce and mirin; simmer until vegetables are tender.

Hōrensō Gomaae (Spinach with Sesame Sauce)

 4 servings   20 Mins   Kcal : 80 Fat: 5g carbs : 5g protein : 8g

Hōrensō Gomaae is a classic Japanese side dish featuring blanched spinach dressed in a savory sesame sauce.

INGREDIENTS

- **1 lb spinach, blanched**
- **2 tablespoons soy sauce**
- **1 tablespoon sugar**
- **2 tablespoons sesame seeds, ground**
- **1 tablespoon mirin**

INSTRUCTIONS

1. Squeeze excess water from blanched spinach.
2. Mix soy sauce, sugar, ground sesame seeds, and mirin.
3. Toss spinach in the sesame sauce.

Kuri Kinton (Sweet Chestnut Purée)

 4 servings   40 Mins   Kcal : 180   Fat: 1g carbs : 45g protein : 2g

Kuri Kinton is a traditional Japanese sweet featuring sweetened chestnut purée, creating a delightful confection.

INGREDIENTS

- **1 lb chestnuts, peeled and cooked**
- **1 cup sugar**
- **1/2 cup water**

INSTRUCTIONS

1. Cook peeled chestnuts until soft.
2. Blend with sugar and water until smooth.

Cherry Blossom Mochi (Sakura Mochi)

 4 servings   40 Mins   Kcal : 150 Fat: 0g carbs : 35 g protein : 2g

Cherry Blossom Mochi, or Sakura Mochi, is a springtime Japanese sweet featuring sweet red bean paste wrapped in a soft mochi skin.

INGREDIENTS

- **Mochi rice flour**
- **Red bean paste**
- **Salted cherry leaves (sakura leaves)**
- **Food coloring (optional)**

INSTRUCTIONS

1. Mix mochi rice flour with water and food coloring (optional).
2. Steam or microwave until the mochi is cooked.
3. Divide the mochi into portions and flatten each portion.
4. Place a small amount of red bean paste in the center and wrap the mochi around it.
5. If available, wrap each mochi in a salted cherry leaf for an authentic touch.

Anmitsu (Japanese Agar Jelly Dessert)

 4 servings   30 Mins   Kcal : 180   Fat: 1 g carbs : 40g protein : 2 g

Anmitsu is a delightful Japanese dessert featuring agar jelly cubes, sweet red bean paste, fruits, and a drizzle of kuromitsu syrup.

INGREDIENTS

- Agar jelly cubes
- Sweet red bean paste
- Mixed fruits (peaches, strawberries, kiwi)
- Kuromitsu syrup (brown sugar syrup)
- Anko (sweetened red bean paste) for topping

INSTRUCTIONS

1. Arrange agar jelly cubes, sweet red bean paste, and mixed fruits in a bowl.
2. Drizzle with kuromitsu syrup and top with anko.

Imagawayaki (Sweet Red Bean-filled Pancakes)

 4 servings   30 Mins   Kcal : 180   Fat: 3g carbs : 40g protein : 0g

Imagawayaki are round, pancake-like treats filled with sweet red bean paste, creating a delightful street food experience.

INGREDIENTS

- 2 cups all-purpose flour
- 1/2 cup sugar
- 1 teaspoon baking powder
- 1 cup water
- Sweet red bean paste

INSTRUCTIONS

1. Whisk together flour, sugar, baking powder, and water to make a batter.
2. Heat an imagawayaki pan, pour in the batter, add a spoonful of red bean paste, and cover with more batter.
3. Cook until golden on both sides.

Yatsuhashi (Cinnamon-flavored Confection)

 12 servings   1 Hour   Kcal : 120 Fat: 1 g carbs : 28g protein : 2 g

Yatsuhashi is a traditional Japanese sweet from Kyoto, often made with glutinous rice flour and flavored with cinnamon.

INGREDIENTS

- **2 cups glutinous rice flour**
- **1 cup sugar**
- **1 teaspoon cinnamon powder**
- **Water**
- **Kinako (roasted soybean flour) for coating**

INSTRUCTIONS

1. Mix glutinous rice flour, sugar, and cinnamon powder.
2. Gradually add water to form a dough.
3. Roll out the dough, cut into triangles, and dust with kinako.

Thai Cuisine

Chicken Satay with Peanut Sauce

 4 servings   45 Mins   Kcal : 300   Fat: 15g   carbs : 15g   protein : 25g

Chicken Satay is a classic Thai street food featuring skewered and grilled chicken served with a flavorful peanut sauce.

INGREDIENTS

- **1 lb chicken breast, sliced into strips**
- 1/4 cup soy sauce
- 2 tablespoons fish sauce
- 1 tablespoon curry powder
- 2 tablespoons brown sugar
- 1 tablespoon minced garlic
- Bamboo skewers, soaked in water
- For Peanut Sauce:
- 1/2 cup peanut butter
- 2 tablespoons soy sauce
- 1 tablespoon lime juice
- 1 tablespoon brown sugar
- 1 teaspoon minced garlic
- Water to thin

INSTRUCTIONS

1. In a bowl, mix soy sauce, fish sauce, curry powder, brown sugar, and minced garlic.
2. Marinate chicken strips in the mixture for at least 30 minutes.
3. Thread marinated chicken onto soaked bamboo skewers.
4. Grill until fully cooked.
5. For peanut sauce, mix peanut butter, soy sauce, lime juice, brown sugar, and garlic. Thin with water to desired consistency.
6. Serve grilled chicken satay with peanut sauce.

Thai Basil Fried Rice

 4 servings   30 Mins   Kcal : 400   Fat: 15g carbs : 15g protein : 20g

Thai Basil Fried Rice is a savory and aromatic dish with jasmine rice, Thai basil, and a blend of spices.

INGREDIENTS

- 3 cups cooked jasmine rice, chilled
- 1 cup chicken or pork, diced
- 1 cup Thai basil leaves
- 1/2 cup bell peppers, diced
- 1/2 cup onions, diced
- 3 tablespoons soy sauce
- 2 tablespoons oyster sauce
- 1 tablespoon fish sauce
- 1 tablespoon sugar
- 2 tablespoons vegetable oil
- 3 cloves garlic, minced
- 2 red chilies, sliced (optional)
- Fried eggs for serving (optional)

INSTRUCTIONS

1. Heat oil in a wok; sauté garlic until fragrant.
2. Add chicken or pork, cook until browned.
3. Add onions and bell peppers; stir-fry until vegetables are tender.
4. Stir in chilled rice, soy sauce, oyster sauce, fish sauce, and sugar.
5. Toss in Thai basil leaves and sliced chilies.
6. Serve hot, topped with a fried egg if desired.

Larb Gai (Minced Chicken Salad)

 4 servings   25 Mins   Kcal : 250 Fat: 10g carbs : 20g protein : 20g

Larb Gai is a Thai salad with minced chicken, fresh herbs, and a zesty dressing.

INGREDIENTS

- **1 lb ground chicken**
- **2 tablespoons rice powder**
- **2 tablespoons fish sauce**
- **2 tablespoons lime juice**
- **1 tablespoon chili flakes**
- **1 teaspoon sugar**
- **1/2 cup mint leaves, chopped**
- **1/2 cup cilantro, chopped**
- **1/4 cup green onions, sliced**
- **Lettuce leaves for serving**

INSTRUCTIONS

1. Cook ground chicken until browned; drain excess liquid.
2. In a bowl, mix rice powder, fish sauce, lime juice, chili flakes, and sugar.
3. Add the cooked chicken to the mixture.
4. Stir in mint leaves, cilantro, and green onions.
5. Serve in lettuce leaves as wraps.

Drunken Noodles (Pad Kee Mao)

 4 servings 230 Mins Kcal : 350   Fat: 50g carbs : 10g protein : 15g

Drunken Noodles, or Pad Kee Mao, is a spicy Thai stir-fried noodle dish with a rich soy and chili-based sauce.

INGREDIENTS

- **8 oz wide rice noodles, cooked**
- **1 cup chicken or tofu, sliced**
- **1 cup bell peppers, sliced**
- **1/2 cup Thai basil leaves**
- **3 tablespoons soy sauce**
- **2 tablespoons oyster sauce**
- **1 tablespoon fish sauce**
- **1 tablespoon sugar**
- **2 tablespoons vegetable oil**
- **3 cloves garlic, minced**
- **2 red chilies, sliced**
- **Lime wedges for serving**

INSTRUCTIONS

1. Heat oil in a wok; sauté garlic until fragrant.
2. Add chicken or tofu, cook until browned.
3. Stir in bell peppers and cook until tender.
4. Add cooked rice noodles, soy sauce, oyster sauce, fish sauce, and sugar.
5. Toss in Thai basil leaves and sliced chilies.
6. Serve hot with lime wedges.

Pineapple Fried Rice

 4 servings   25 Mins   Kcal : 450 Fat: 60g carbs : 20g protein : 18g

Pineapple Fried Rice is a sweet and savory Thai dish with a tropical twist.

INGREDIENTS

- 3 cups cooked jasmine rice, chilled
- 1 cup chicken or shrimp, cooked
- 1 cup pineapple, diced
- 1/2 cup cashews, toasted
- 1/2 cup raisins
- 1/2 cup peas
- 2 tablespoons soy sauce
- 1 tablespoon fish sauce
- 1 tablespoon curry powder
- 1 tablespoon sugar
- 2 tablespoons vegetable oil
- 3 cloves garlic, minced
- 2 green onions, sliced

INSTRUCTIONS

1. Heat oil in a wok; sauté garlic until fragrant.
2. Add chicken or shrimp, cook until browned.
3. Stir in pineapple, cashews, raisins, and peas; cook until heated through.
4. Add chilled rice, soy sauce, fish sauce, curry powder, and sugar.
5. Toss the mixture until well combined.
6. Top with toasted cashews and sliced green onions.
7. Serve hot as a flavorful side dish or main course.

Thai Yellow Curry with Potatoes

 4 servings   35 Mins   Kcal : 400   Fat: 25g carbs : 30g protein : 20g

Thai Yellow Curry with Potatoes is a comforting and aromatic curry with a perfect balance of flavors.

INGREDIENTS

- 1 lb chicken or tofu, cut into cubes
- 2 potatoes, peeled and diced
- 1 can (13.5 oz) coconut milk
- 2 tablespoons yellow curry paste
- 1 tablespoon fish sauce
- 1 tablespoon soy sauce
- 1 tablespoon brown sugar
- 1 cup broccoli florets
- 1 red bell pepper, sliced
- Fresh cilantro for garnish
- Lime wedges for serving
- Cooked jasmine rice for serving

INSTRUCTIONS

1. In a pot, simmer coconut milk, yellow curry paste, fish sauce, soy sauce, and brown sugar.
2. Add chicken or tofu and potatoes; cook until potatoes are tender.
3. Stir in broccoli and red bell pepper; cook until vegetables are crisp-tender.
4. Garnish with fresh cilantro.
5. Serve over jasmine rice with lime wedges on the side.

Gaeng Keow Wan Gai (Green Curry Chicken)

 4 servings 30 Mins Kcal : 450 Fat: 30g carbs : 20g protein : 25g

Gaeng Keow Wan Gai, or Green Curry Chicken, is a flavorful Thai curry with tender chicken, vegetables, and aromatic green curry paste.

INGREDIENTS

- 1 lb chicken thighs, boneless and skinless, sliced
- 1 can (13.5 oz) coconut milk
- 2 tablespoons green curry paste
- 1 tablespoon fish sauce
- 1 tablespoon brown sugar
- 1 cup bamboo shoots
- 1 cup bell peppers, sliced
- 1 cup Thai basil leaves
- Fresh cilantro for garnish
- Cooked jasmine rice for serving

INSTRUCTIONS

1. In a pot, simmer coconut milk, green curry paste, fish sauce, and brown sugar.
2. Add sliced chicken; cook until chicken is cooked through.
3. Stir in bamboo shoots and bell peppers; cook until vegetables are tender.
4. Toss in Thai basil leaves.
5. Garnish with fresh cilantro.
6. Serve hot over jasmine rice.

Thai Iced Tea

 4 servings 15 Mins Kcal : 80   Fat: 3g carbs : 15g protein : 1g

Thai Iced Tea is a sweet and creamy beverage with strong brewed black tea and condensed milk.

INGREDIENTS

- **4 black tea bags**
- **4 cups boiling water**
- **1/2 cup sweetened condensed milk**
- **Ice cubes**

INSTRUCTIONS

1. Steep black tea bags in boiling water for 5-7 minutes; let it cool.
2. Fill glasses with ice cubes.
3. Pour the brewed tea over the ice.
4. Add sweetened condensed milk and stir well.
5. Adjust sweetness according to taste.
6. Serve chilled and enjoy this refreshing Thai beverage.

Khao Pad Tom Yum (Tom Yum Fried Rice)

 4 servings   25 Mins   Kcal : 350 Fat: 10g carbs : 50g protein : 15g

Khao Pad Tom Yum is a delightful twist on traditional fried rice with the bold flavors of Tom Yum soup.

INGREDIENTS

- **3 cups cooked jasmine rice, chilled**
- **1 cup shrimp, cooked and peeled**
- 1/2 cup pineapple, diced
- 1/2 cup cherry tomatoes, halved
- 1/4 cup green onions, sliced
- 2 tablespoons Tom Yum paste
- 1 tablespoon fish sauce
- 1 tablespoon soy sauce
- 1 tablespoon sugar
- 2 tablespoons vegetable oil
- 3 cloves garlic, minced
- 2 red chilies, sliced (optional)

INSTRUCTIONS

1. Heat oil in a wok; sauté garlic until fragrant.
2. Add shrimp, cook until pink and cooked through.
3. Stir in pineapple, cherry tomatoes, and green onions; cook until heated through.
4. Add chilled rice, Tom Yum paste, fish sauce, soy sauce, and sugar.
5. Toss until well combined.
6. Top with sliced red chilies if desired.
7. Serve hot as a delicious and aromatic fried rice.

Pad Ped Moo Krob (Crispy Pork Belly with Red Curry)

 4 servings   40 Mins   Kcal : 500 Fat: 40g carbs : 15g protein : 20g

Pad Ped Moo Krob is a mouthwatering Thai dish with crispy pork belly cooked in a spicy and aromatic red curry sauce.

INGREDIENTS

- 1 lb pork belly, skin-on, cut into bite-sized pieces
- 2 tablespoons red curry paste
- 1 can (13.5 oz) coconut milk
- 2 tablespoons fish sauce
- 1 tablespoon soy sauce
- 1 tablespoon sugar
- Thai basil leaves for garnish
- Sliced red chilies for garnish

INSTRUCTIONS

1. Fry pork belly until crispy; drain excess oil.
2. In a pan, simmer coconut milk, red curry paste, fish sauce, soy sauce, and sugar.
3. Add crispy pork belly to the sauce; coat well.
4. Cook until the sauce thickens.
5. Garnish with Thai basil leaves and sliced red chilies.
6. Serve hot over jasmine rice.

Pla Rad Prik (Crispy Fish with Chili Sauce)

 4 servings   23 Mins   Kcal : 300   Fat: 15g   carbs : 20g   protein : 20g

Pla Rad Prik is a delectable Thai dish featuring crispy fried fish served with a spicy chili sauce.

INGREDIENTS

- 4 fish fillets (tilapia or snapper)
- 1 cup all-purpose flour
- 2 tablespoons red curry paste
- 2 tablespoons fish sauce
- 1 tablespoon soy sauce
- 1 tablespoon sugar
- Vegetable oil for frying
- Sliced green onions for garnish
- Sesame seeds for garnish

INSTRUCTIONS

1. Dredge fish fillets in flour; fry until golden brown and crispy.
2. In a bowl, mix red curry paste, fish sauce, soy sauce, and sugar.
3. Toss fried fish in the sauce until well coated.
4. Garnish with sliced green onions and sesame seeds.
5. Serve hot with jasmine rice.

Thai Coconut Soup (Tom Kha)

 4 servings 35 Mins Kcal : 350   Fat: 25g carbs : 15g protein : 15g

Tom Kha is a rich and tangy Thai coconut soup with a harmonious blend of coconut milk, lemongrass, and aromatic herbs.

INGREDIENTS

- 1 lb chicken or tofu, sliced
- 1 can (13.5 oz) coconut milk
- 3 cups chicken or vegetable broth
- 2 lemongrass stalks, bruised
- 3 kaffir lime leaves
- 1 tablespoon galangal, sliced
- 1 tablespoon fish sauce
- 1 tablespoon soy sauce
- 1 tablespoon sugar
- 1 cup mushrooms, sliced
- 1 cup cherry tomatoes, halved
- Fresh cilantro for garnish
- Lime wedges for serving

INSTRUCTIONS

1. In a pot, simmer coconut milk, broth, lemongrass, kaffir lime leaves, galangal, fish sauce, soy sauce, and sugar.
2. Add sliced chicken or tofu; cook until cooked through.
3. Stir in mushrooms and cherry tomatoes; cook until vegetables are tender.
4. Discard lemongrass, kaffir lime leaves, and galangal.
5. Garnish with fresh cilantro.
6. Serve hot with lime wedges.

Mango and Sticky Rice Pancakes

 4 servings   40 Mins   Kcal : 350   Fat: 10g carbs : 65g protein : 5g

Mango and Sticky Rice Pancakes are a delightful Thai dessert featuring sweet mango, coconut-infused sticky rice, and a pancake wrap.

INGREDIENTS

- **1 cup glutinous rice, soaked and cooked**
- **1/2 cup coconut milk**
- **1/4 cup sugar**
- **4 ripe mangoes, peeled and sliced**
- **Pancake batter**
- **Butter or oil for cooking**
- **Sesame seeds for garnish**

INSTRUCTIONS

1. In a bowl, mix cooked glutinous rice, coconut milk, and sugar.
2. Lay out pancake batter and spoon rice mixture onto pancakes.
3. Wrap pancakes around rice and seal edges.
4. Cook pancakes until golden brown.
5. Serve with sliced mangoes and sprinkle with sesame seeds.

Pad Thai (Thai Stir-Fried Noodles)

 4 servings   30 Mins   Kcal : 400   Fat: 15g carbs : 50g protein : 20g

Pad Thai is a classic Thai street food dish featuring stir-fried rice noodles with a perfect balance of sweet, sour, and savory flavors.

INGREDIENTS

- **8 oz rice noodles**
- **1/2 lb shrimp, peeled and deveined**
- **1 cup tofu, cubed**
- **2 eggs**
- **1 cup bean sprouts**
- **3 green onions, chopped**
- **1/4 cup crushed peanuts**
- **1 lime, cut into wedges**
- **Pad Thai sauce (tamarind paste, fish sauce, sugar, chili flakes)**

INSTRUCTIONS

1. Soak rice noodles in warm water until softened; drain.
2. Stir-fry shrimp, tofu, and eggs.
3. Add noodles and Pad Thai sauce; toss to combine.
4. Top with bean sprouts, green onions, peanuts, and lime.

Tom Yum Goong (Thai Hot and Sour Shrimp Soup)

 4 servings   25 Mins   Kcal : 150   Fat: 5g carbs : 10g protein : 15g

Tom Yum Goong is a quintessential Thai soup known for its bold and invigorating flavors, featuring shrimp, mushrooms, and aromatic herbs.

INGREDIENTS

- 1 lb shrimp, peeled and deveined
- 4 cups chicken or vegetable broth
- 1 lemongrass stalk, bruised
- 3 kaffir lime leaves
- 2 tomatoes, quartered
- 1 onion, sliced
- 1 cup mushrooms, sliced
- 2 Thai bird chilies, minced
- 2 tablespoons fish sauce
- 1 tablespoon lime juice
- Fresh cilantro for garnish

INSTRUCTIONS

1. Bring broth to a boil with lemongrass and lime leaves.
2. Add shrimp, tomatoes, onion, mushrooms, and chilies.
3. Season with fish sauce and lime juice.
4. Simmer until shrimp are cooked; garnish with cilantro.

Som Tum (Green Papaya Salad)

 4 servings   20 Mins   Kcal : 120   Fat: 6g carbs : 15g protein : 3g

Som Tum is a refreshing and spicy Thai salad featuring shredded green papaya, cherry tomatoes, peanuts, and a zesty dressing.

INGREDIENTS

- 1 green papaya, peeled and shredded
- 1 cup cherry tomatoes, halved
- 2 cloves garlic, minced
- 2 Thai bird chilies, minced
- 2 tablespoons fish sauce
- 1 tablespoon palm sugar
- 1 tablespoon lime juice
- 2 tablespoons roasted peanuts
- Fresh cilantro for garnish

INSTRUCTIONS

1. In a mortar, pound garlic and chilies.
2. Add fish sauce, palm sugar, and lime juice.
3. Toss shredded papaya, tomatoes, and dressing.
4. Garnish with peanuts and cilantro.

Massaman Curry Beef

 4 servings   40 Mins   Kcal : 350   Fat: 25g carbs : 15g protein : 20g

Massaman Curry Beef is a rich and flavorful Thai curry with tender beef, potatoes, and peanuts in a fragrant Massaman curry sauce.

INGREDIENTS

- 1 lb beef stew meat, cubed
- 1 can (14 oz) coconut milk
- 2 tablespoons Massaman curry paste
- 1 onion, sliced
- 2 potatoes, peeled and diced
- 1/2 cup roasted peanuts
- Fish sauce and palm sugar to taste

INSTRUCTIONS

1. Cook Massaman curry paste in coconut milk until aromatic.
2. Add beef, onion, potatoes, and peanuts.
3. Simmer until beef is tender.
4. Season with fish sauce and palm sugar.

Panang Curry with Tofu

 4 servings   30 Mins   Kcal : 250 Fat: 25g carbs : 20g protein : 15g

Panang Curry with Tofu is a creamy and mildly spicy Thai curry with tofu, bell peppers, and a luscious Panang curry sauce.

INGREDIENTS

- 1 block (14 oz) firm tofu, cubed
- 1 can (14 oz) coconut milk
- 2 tablespoons Panang curry paste
- 1 red bell pepper, sliced
- 1 cup green beans, trimmed
- Kaffir lime leaves for garnish
- Fish sauce and palm sugar to taste

INSTRUCTIONS

1. Cook Panang curry paste in coconut milk until fragrant.
2. Add tofu, bell pepper, and green beans.
3. Simmer until vegetables are tender.
4. Season with fish sauce and palm sugar.
5. Garnish with kaffir lime leaves.

Thai Basil Chicken (Pad Krapow Gai)

 4 servings   20 Mins   Kcal : 250   Fat: 15g   carbs : 10g   protein : 20g

Thai Basil Chicken, or Pad Krapow Gai, is a quick and flavorful stir-fry with ground chicken, Thai basil, and a savory sauce.

INGREDIENTS

- 1 lb ground chicken
- 2 cups Thai basil leaves
- 3 cloves garlic, minced
- 2 Thai bird chilies, minced
- 2 tablespoons fish sauce
- 1 tablespoon soy sauce
- 1 teaspoon oyster sauce
- 1 teaspoon sugar
- Vegetable oil for cooking

INSTRUCTIONS

1. Heat oil and sauté garlic and chilies until fragrant.
2. Add ground chicken; cook until browned.
3. Stir in fish sauce, soy sauce, oyster sauce, and sugar.
4. Add Thai basil leaves; stir until wilted.

Thai Iced Coffee

 4 servings   10 Mins   Kcal : 120   Fat: 5g   carbs : 15g protein : 2g

Thai Iced Coffee is a sweet and creamy beverage made with strong brewed coffee, sweetened condensed milk, and ice.

INGREDIENTS

- **2 cups strong brewed coffee, cooled**
- **1/2 cup sweetened condensed milk**
- **Ice cubes**

INSTRUCTIONS

1. Mix brewed coffee with sweetened condensed milk.
2. Pour over ice and stir until well combined.

Crying Tiger Beef (Suea Rong Hai)

 4 servings   40 Mins   Kcal : 300   Fat: 15g carbs : 10g protein : 25g

Crying Tiger Beef is a popular Thai grilled beef dish served with a spicy dipping sauce, bringing bold flavors to your barbecue.

INGREDIENTS

- **1 lb beef sirloin or flank steak**
- **2 tablespoons fish sauce**
- **2 tablespoons soy sauce**
- **1 tablespoon oyster sauce**
- **1 tablespoon sugar**
- **2 cloves garlic, minced**
- **Thai bird chilies for spice**

INSTRUCTIONS

1. Mix fish sauce, soy sauce, oyster sauce, sugar, and garlic.
2. Marinate beef in the mixture for 30 minutes.
3. Grill beef to desired doneness; slice.
4. Serve with Thai bird chilies on the side.

Papaya Salad with Salted Crab (Som Tum Poo Ma)

 4 servings   30 Mins   Kcal : 180   Fat: 5g carbs : 25g protein : 10g

Papaya Salad with Salted Crab is a unique and flavorful Thai salad featuring shredded green papaya, tomatoes, chilies, and salted crab.

INGREDIENTS

- 1 green papaya, peeled and shredded
- 1 cup cherry tomatoes, halved
- 2 Thai bird chilies, minced
- 2 tablespoons fish sauce
- 1 tablespoon palm sugar
- 1 tablespoon lime juice
- 1/2 cup salted crab, cleaned and shredded

INSTRUCTIONS

1. Pound chilies in a mortar; add fish sauce, palm sugar, and lime juice.
2. Toss shredded papaya, tomatoes, and dressing.
3. Add shredded salted crab; mix well.

Thai Basil Eggplant Stir-Fry

 4 servings   25 Mins   Kcal : 200   Fat: 10g carbs : 3g protein : 10g

Thai Basil Eggplant Stir-Fry is a vegetarian delight featuring eggplant, tofu, and Thai basil in a savory and spicy sauce.

INGREDIENTS

- 2 Japanese eggplants, sliced
- 1 cup firm tofu, cubed
- 2 tablespoons vegetable oil
- 3 cloves garlic, minced
- 2 Thai bird chilies, minced
- 2 tablespoons soy sauce
- 1 tablespoon oyster sauce
- 1 tablespoon fish sauce
- 1 teaspoon sugar
- Fresh Thai basil leaves for garnish

INSTRUCTIONS

1. Stir-fry eggplant and tofu in oil until golden.
2. Add garlic and chilies; sauté until fragrant.
3. Mix soy sauce, oyster sauce, fish sauce, and sugar; add to the pan.
4. Stir in Thai basil leaves; cook until wilted.

Korean Cuisine

Kimbap (Korean Seaweed Rice Rolls)

 5 servings   45 Mins   Kcal : 280 Fat: 3g carbs : 55g protein : 7g

Kimbap, a Korean staple, is a delicious and portable dish featuring seasoned rice and various ingredients rolled in seaweed. It's often compared to sushi, but the flavors are distinctively Korean.

INGREDIENTS

- **2 cups sushi rice, cooked and seasoned with rice vinegar, sugar, and salt**
- **5 sheets of roasted seaweed (gim)**
- **1/2 pound imitation crab or cooked shrimp, sliced**
- **1 carrot, julienned**
- **1 cucumber, julienned**
- **5 strips of pickled yellow radish (danmuji)**
- **5 slices of ham**
- **Sesame oil**
- **Soy sauce for dipping**

INSTRUCTIONS

1. Place a bamboo sushi rolling mat on a flat surface and put a sheet of plastic wrap on top.
2. Lay one sheet of seaweed on the plastic wrap.
3. Wet your hands to prevent sticking, then spread a thin layer of rice on the seaweed, leaving about an inch at the top.
4. Arrange the filling ingredients horizontally on the rice.
5. Roll the seaweed tightly from the bottom using the sushi mat.
6. Wet the top edge with water to seal the roll.
7. Repeat for the remaining sheets.
8. Brush sesame oil on the rolls and slice into bite-sized pieces.
9. Serve kimbap with soy sauce for dipping. It's great for picnics, lunchboxes, or as a snack.

Sundubu Jjigae (Soft Tofu Stew)

 4 servings   35 Mins   Kcal : 220 Fat: 12g carbs : 14g protein : 15g

Sundubu Jjigae is a comforting Korean stew known for its rich, spicy broth and silky soft tofu. It's a popular choice, especially during colder seasons.

INGREDIENTS

- 1 pack of soft tofu (sundubu)
- 1/2 cup of minced pork or beef
- 1/2 cup of chopped kimchi
- 1/2 cup of sliced mushrooms
- 1/4 cup of diced onion
- 2 cloves of garlic, minced
- 1 tablespoon of gochugaru (Korean red pepper flakes)
- 1 tablespoon of gochujang (Korean red pepper paste)
- 1 tablespoon of soy sauce
- 1 tablespoon of sesame oil
- 4 cups of anchovy or vegetable broth
- 1 green onion, chopped
- Salt and pepper to taste

INSTRUCTIONS

1. In a pot, sauté the garlic and onions until fragrant.
2. Add the minced meat and cook until browned.
3. Stir in gochugaru, gochujang, and soy sauce.
4. Pour in the broth and bring it to a gentle boil.
5. Carefully add the tofu, kimchi, mushrooms, and cook for 8-10 minutes.
6. Season with salt and pepper, and drizzle with sesame oil.
7. Garnish with chopped green onions before serving.
8. Serve Sundubu Jjigae hot with a bowl of steamed rice. It's a complete meal on its own.

Dak Galbi (Spicy Stir-Fried Chicken)

 4 servings   1 Hour   Kcal : 380   Fat: 12g   carbs : 45g   protein : 25g

Dak Galbi is a vibrant and spicy Korean dish featuring marinated chicken stir-fried with an array of vegetables. The combination of gochujang and other seasonings gives it a flavorful kick.

INGREDIENTS

- 1 pound boneless, skinless chicken thighs, thinly sliced
- 2 cups cabbage, shredded
- 1 sweet potato, thinly sliced
- 1 carrot, julienned
- 1 onion, thinly sliced
- 3 green onions, cut into 2-inch pieces
- 3 tablespoons gochujang (Korean red pepper paste)
- 2 tablespoons soy sauce
- 1 tablespoon sugar
- 1 tablespoon minced garlic
- 1 tablespoon sesame oil
- 1 tablespoon vegetable oil
- 1 teaspoon grated ginger
- Sesame seeds for garnish
- Cooked rice for serving

INSTRUCTIONS

1. In a bowl, mix the gochujang, soy sauce, sugar, garlic, sesame oil, and grated ginger to create the marinade.
2. Add the sliced chicken to the marinade and let it sit for at least 30 minutes.
3. Heat vegetable oil in a large pan or wok over medium heat.
4. Add marinated chicken and stir-fry until cooked through.
5. Add vegetables and continue stir-frying until they are tender yet crisp.
6. Garnish with sesame seeds and green onions.
7. Serve over steamed rice.
8. Dak Galbi is best enjoyed with a side of rice and shared with family or friends.

Pajeon (Green Onion Pancakes)

 6 servings   30 mins   Kcal : 220 Fat: 8g carbs : 30g protein : 8g

Pajeon, or green onion pancakes, are a popular Korean appetizer or side dish. They are savory pancakes made with a simple batter and loaded with green onions, giving them a deliciously crispy texture.

INGREDIENTS

- **2 cups all-purpose flour**
- **2 cups cold water**
- **1 egg**
- **1 bunch green onions, finely chopped**
- **1/2 cup seafood (optional), such as small shrimp or squid, chopped**
- **1/4 cup soy sauce**
- **1 tablespoon sesame oil**
- **1 tablespoon vegetable oil**
- **Salt and pepper to taste**
- **Vegetable oil for frying**

INSTRUCTIONS

1. In a bowl, whisk together the flour, cold water, and egg until you have a smooth batter.
2. Add chopped green onions and seafood (if using) to the batter. Mix well.
3. Heat vegetable oil in a large skillet or pan over medium heat.
4. Ladle the batter into the pan, spreading it evenly to form a pancake.
5. Cook for 3-4 minutes on each side or until golden brown and crispy.
6. Combine soy sauce and sesame oil for dipping sauce.
7. Cut Pajeon into slices and serve hot with the dipping sauce. It's excellent as an appetizer or snack.

Kimchi Pancakes

 4 servings   30 Mins   Kcal : 220   Fat: 12g carbs : 23g protein :5g

Kimchi pancakes are a delightful Korean dish that combines the tangy and spicy flavors of kimchi with a crispy pancake. They make for a tasty appetizer or a side dish.

INGREDIENTS

- **1 cup all-purpose flour**
- **1 cup water**
- **1 egg**
- **1 cup kimchi, chopped**
- **1/4 cup kimchi juice**
- **2 tablespoons soy sauce**
- **1 tablespoon sesame oil**
- **2 green onions, finely chopped**
- **1/4 cup vegetable oil (for frying)**
- **Sesame seeds for garnish**
- **Dipping sauce: soy sauce mixed with a splash of rice vinegar**

INSTRUCTIONS

1. In a bowl, whisk together flour, water, egg, soy sauce, and sesame oil to create the batter.
2. Add chopped kimchi, kimchi juice, and green onions to the batter. Mix well.
3. Heat vegetable oil in a skillet over medium heat.
4. Spoon the batter into the skillet, spreading it to form a pancake.
5. Cook for 3-4 minutes on each side until golden brown and crispy.
6. Garnish with sesame seeds.
7. Mix soy sauce with rice vinegar for the dipping sauce.
8. Serve Kimchi Pancakes hot with the dipping sauce. They are perfect for sharing or as a tasty side dish.

Doenjang Jjigae (Soybean Paste Stew)

 4 servings    40 Mins   Kcal : 120   Fat: 7g carbs : 10g protein : 5g

Doenjang Jjigae is a classic Korean stew known for its hearty flavor derived from fermented soybean paste. Packed with vegetables and often featuring tofu or meat, it's a comforting dish enjoyed year-round.

INGREDIENTS

- 1/2 cup doenjang (Korean soybean paste)
- 1/2 cup tofu, cubed
- 1/2 cup zucchini, sliced
- 1/2 cup Korean radish or daikon, sliced
- 1/2 cup onion, sliced
- 2 cloves garlic, minced
- 1 green chili pepper, sliced (optional, for spice)
- 1 tablespoon vegetable oil
- 4 cups anchovy or vegetable broth
- 1 tablespoon soy sauce
- 1 tablespoon sesame oil
- 1 tablespoon gochugaru (Korean red pepper flakes) (optional)
- 1 green onion, chopped (for garnish)

INSTRUCTIONS

1. In a pot, heat vegetable oil over medium heat. Add garlic and sauté until fragrant.
2. Add sliced onions, zucchini, and radish. Cook until slightly softened.
3. Pour in the broth and bring it to a simmer.
4. Dissolve doenjang in a ladle of the broth, then add it to the pot.
5. Add tofu and green chili pepper (if using).
6. Season with soy sauce, sesame oil, and gochugaru (if desired).
7. Simmer for 15-20 minutes until the vegetables are tender.
8. Garnish with chopped green onions before serving.
9. Serve Doenjang Jjigae hot with a bowl of steamed rice. It's a soul-warming dish perfect for chilly days.

Tteokbokki (Spicy Rice Cake)

 4 servings   50 Mins   Kcal : 380   Fat:8g carbs : 60g protein : 10g

Tteokbokki is a popular Korean street food known for its addictive sweet and spicy sauce coating chewy rice cakes. This dish offers a unique combination of textures and flavors that make it a favorite among locals and international food enthusiasts alike.

INGREDIENTS

- **1 pound cylindrical rice cakes (tteok)**
- **2 cups Korean fish cake, sliced**
- **3 cups cabbage, thinly sliced**
- **4 cups anchovy or beef broth**
- **1/2 cup gochujang (Korean red pepper paste)**
- **2 tablespoons gochugaru (Korean red pepper flakes)**
- **3 tablespoons soy sauce**
- **2 tablespoons sugar**
- **2 tablespoons vegetable oil**
- **2 cloves garlic, minced**
- **1 hard-boiled egg (optional, for garnish)**
- **Sesame seeds and chopped green onions (for garnish)**

INSTRUCTIONS

1. Soak rice cakes in warm water for 30 minutes to soften.
2. In a pot, heat vegetable oil and sauté garlic until fragrant.
3. Add gochujang, gochugaru, and soy sauce. Stir well.
4. Pour in the broth and bring it to a boil.
5. Add rice cakes, fish cakes, cabbage, and sugar. Simmer until the rice cakes are tender.
6. Adjust the seasoning to taste.
7. Garnish with sesame seeds, chopped green onions, and sliced hard-boiled egg if desired.
8. Serve Tteokbokki hot as a snack or a main dish. It's commonly enjoyed with a side of pickled radishes.

Bossam (Pork Belly Wraps)

 6 servings   1 Hour 15 Mins   Kcal : 320 Fat: 28g carbs : 5 protein : 15g

Bossam is a traditional Korean dish where thinly sliced, boiled pork belly is served with a variety of condiments and wrapped in lettuce leaves. It's a customizable and flavorful dish often enjoyed with family and friends.

INGREDIENTS

- **1.5 pounds pork belly**
- **1 onion, peeled and halved**
- **1 leek, cleaned and halved**
- **1 knob of ginger, sliced**
- **4 cloves garlic, crushed**
- **2 bay leaves**
- **1 tablespoon soybean paste (doenjang)**
- **1 tablespoon sesame oil**
- **1 tablespoon soy sauce**
- **2 teaspoons sugar**
- **Lettuce leaves, for wrapping**
- **Ssamjang (thick, spicy paste) for serving**
- **Garlic cloves, sliced**
- **Green onions, sliced**
- **Fresh red and green chili peppers, sliced**

INSTRUCTIONS

1. In a large pot, bring water to a boil and add pork belly, onion, leek, ginger, garlic, and bay leaves.
2. Simmer until the pork is cooked through, about 45-60 minutes.
3. While boiling, mix soybean paste, sesame oil, soy sauce, and sugar to create a dipping sauce.
4. Once the pork is tender, remove it from the pot and thinly slice.
5. Serve the sliced pork with lettuce leaves and an array of condiments such as ssamjang, sliced garlic, green onions, and chili peppers.
6. To eat, place a slice of pork in a lettuce leaf, add condiments, and wrap it up.
7. Serve Bossam as a communal dish, allowing everyone to create their own wraps. It's often enjoyed with a side of kimchi.

Korean Army Stew (Budae Jjigae)

 4 servings   50 Mins   [Kcal] Kcal : 550   Fat: 25g carbs : 60g protein : 20g

Korean Army Stew, or Budae Jjigae, originated during the Korean War when food was scarce, and locals improvised by using surplus military rations. Today, it's a popular comfort food featuring a spicy broth, various ingredients, and the unique addition of instant ramen noodles.

INGREDIENTS

- **1/2 pound thinly sliced pork belly or pork shoulder**
- **1/2 pound smoked sausage, sliced**
- **1 cup baked beans**
- **1 cup kimchi, chopped**
- **1 cup sliced mushrooms**
- **1 cup tofu, cubed**
- **1 cup sliced rice cakes (tteok)**
- **2 cups cabbage, shredded**
- **4 cups anchovy or beef broth**
- **2 tablespoons gochujang (Korean red pepper paste)**
- **1 tablespoon gochugaru (Korean red pepper flakes)**
- **2 tablespoons soy sauce**
- **2 tablespoons mirin or rice wine**
- **2 cloves garlic, minced**
- **2 green onions, chopped**
- **2 packs instant ramen noodles**
- **Sesame oil for drizzling**

INSTRUCTIONS

1. In a pot, combine broth, gochujang, gochugaru, soy sauce, mirin, and garlic. Bring it to a boil.
2. Add pork, sausage, kimchi, mushrooms, tofu, rice cakes, and cabbage. Simmer until ingredients are cooked.
3. Cook instant ramen noodles separately according to package instructions.
4. Add cooked ramen noodles to the pot and mix well.
5. Garnish with green onions and drizzle with sesame oil before serving.
6. Serve Korean Army Stew hot, family-style. It's a communal dish meant for sharing.

Samgyetang (Ginseng Chicken Soup)

 4 servings   2 Hours 15 Mins   Kcal : 500   Fat: 15g carbs : 60g protein : 30g

Samgyetang is a nourishing Korean soup traditionally consumed during the hot summer months to combat fatigue. It features a whole young chicken stuffed with glutinous rice, garlic, jujubes, and ginseng, creating a hearty and healthful meal.

INGREDIENTS

- **1 whole young chicken (about 3-4 pounds)**
- **1 cup glutinous rice, soaked for 1-2 hours**
- **6-8 cloves garlic, peeled**
- **4 jujubes (Korean dates)**
- **4 slices fresh ginseng or 1 tablespoon dried ginseng**
- **Salt and pepper to taste**
- **8 cups water**
- **Green onions and sesame seeds for garnish**

INSTRUCTIONS

1. Rinse the soaked glutinous rice and stuff it into the cavity of the chicken.
2. Place the stuffed chicken in a pot and add garlic, jujubes, ginseng, salt, and pepper.
3. Pour water over the chicken and bring it to a boil.
4. Reduce the heat to low, cover, and simmer for 1.5 to 2 hours until the chicken is tender.
5. Skim off any impurities that rise to the surface.
6. Garnish with chopped green onions and sesame seeds before serving.
7. Serve Samgyetang hot, typically as a single-serving dish. It's believed to boost energy and vitality.

Hobak Jeon (Zucchini Pancakes)

 4 servings   30 Mins   Kcal : 180   Fat: 7g carbs : 25g protein : 5g

Hobak Jeon, or zucchini pancakes, is a popular Korean appetizer or side dish. These savory pancakes are made with thinly sliced zucchini coated in a light batter and pan-fried until crispy. They are enjoyed for their delightful crunch and subtle sweetness.

INGREDIENTS

- **2 medium-sized zucchinis**
- **1 cup all-purpose flour**
- **1/2 cup water**
- **1 egg**
- **1 teaspoon salt**
- **Vegetable oil for frying**
- **Soy sauce for dipping**

INSTRUCTIONS

1. Wash and trim the ends of the zucchinis. Slice them thinly into rounds.
2. In a bowl, whisk together flour, water, egg, and salt to create the pancake batter.
3. Heat vegetable oil in a skillet over medium heat.
4. Dip each zucchini slice into the batter, coating it evenly, and place it in the skillet.
5. Fry until both sides are golden brown and crispy.
6. Place the cooked pancakes on a paper towel to absorb excess oil.
7. Serve hot with soy sauce for dipping.
8. Hobak Jeon can be served as an appetizer, side dish, or part of a Korean meal. It's best enjoyed fresh and hot.

Mul Naengmyeon (Cold Noodle Soup)

 4 servings   25 Mins   Kcal : 300   Fat: 6g carbs : 50g protein : 12g

Mul Naengmyeon is a popular Korean cold noodle dish, perfect for refreshing yourself during hot summer days. It features chewy buckwheat noodles served in an icy broth with tangy flavors, topped with various vegetables and a hard-boiled egg.

INGREDIENTS

- 2 packs of buckwheat noodles (naengmyeon)
- 4 cups beef or vegetable broth, chilled
- 2 tablespoons soy sauce
- 1 tablespoon sugar
- 1 tablespoon rice vinegar
- 1 tablespoon mustard sauce
- 1 teaspoon sesame oil
- 1 cucumber, julienned
- 1 radish, julienned
- 2 hard-boiled eggs, sliced
- Ice cubes (optional)

INSTRUCTIONS

1. Cook the buckwheat noodles according to package instructions. Rinse under cold water and drain.
2. In a bowl, mix chilled broth with soy sauce, sugar, rice vinegar, mustard sauce, and sesame oil to create the soup base.
3. Place a handful of ice cubes in each serving bowl if you prefer an extra chill.
4. Divide the noodles among the bowls and pour the soup over them.
5. Top with julienned cucumber, radish, and sliced hard-boiled eggs.
6. Mul Naengmyeon is traditionally served in individual bowls. Mix the ingredients before eating to enjoy the refreshing combination of flavors.

Korean Seafood Pancake

 4 servings   30 Mins   Kcal : 250   Fat: 12g carbs : 20g protein : 15g

Korean Seafood Pancake, known as Haemul Pajeon, is a savory pancake filled with a variety of seafood and green onions. This crispy and flavorful dish is a popular choice for sharing as an appetizer or snack.

INGREDIENTS

- 1 cup all-purpose flour
- 1 cup water
- 1 egg
- 1 tablespoon soy sauce
- 1 tablespoon sesame oil
- 2 cups mixed seafood (shrimp, squid, and/or mussels), chopped
- 1 cup green onions, sliced
- 1/2 cup onion, thinly sliced
- Vegetable oil for frying
- Soy dipping sauce

INSTRUCTIONS

1. In a bowl, whisk together flour, water, egg, soy sauce, and sesame oil to create the pancake batter.
2. Add chopped seafood, sliced green onions, and sliced onion to the batter. Mix well.
3. Heat vegetable oil in a skillet over medium heat.
4. Pour a ladle of batter into the skillet, spreading it evenly to form a pancake.
5. Cook until the edges are crispy, then flip and cook the other side until golden brown.
6. Repeat for the remaining batter.
7. Cut the pancakes into wedges and serve hot with soy dipping sauce.
8. Korean Seafood Pancake is often served as a shared appetizer or snack. It pairs well with a side of pickled radishes.

Oi Muchim (Spicy Cucumber Salad)

 4 servings   40Mins   Kcal : 300 Fat: 2g carbs : 4g protein : 1g

Oi Muchim, or Spicy Cucumber Salad, is a refreshing Korean side dish that offers a perfect balance of crunch, heat, and tanginess. It's quick to prepare and serves as an excellent accompaniment to a variety of Korean dishes.

INGREDIENTS

- **2 medium-sized cucumbers, thinly sliced**
- **1 tablespoon gochugaru (Korean red pepper flakes)**
- **1 tablespoon soy sauce**
- **1 tablespoon rice vinegar**
- **1 tablespoon sesame oil**
- **1 teaspoon sugar**
- **1 clove garlic, minced**
- **1 teaspoon sesame seeds (optional)**
- **Chopped green onions for garnish**

INSTRUCTIONS

1. Thinly slice the cucumbers and place them in a bowl.
2. In a separate bowl, mix together gochugaru, soy sauce, rice vinegar, sesame oil, sugar, and minced garlic to create the dressing.
3. Pour the dressing over the sliced cucumbers and toss to coat evenly.
4. Let the salad marinate in the refrigerator for at least 30 minutes to allow the flavors to meld.
5. Garnish with sesame seeds and chopped green onions before serving
6. Serve Oi Muchim chilled as a refreshing side dish. It complements spicy and savory Korean main courses.

Kimchi Bokkeumbap (Kimchi Fried Rice)

 4 servings   30 Mins   Kcal : 350 Fat: 8g carbs : 60g protein : 12g

Kimchi Bokkeumbap is a flavorful and satisfying Korean dish that transforms leftover rice into a delicious fried rice with the bold taste of kimchi. This quick and easy recipe is perfect for a quick meal.

INGREDIENTS

- **3 cups cooked rice (preferably day-old)**
- **1 cup kimchi, chopped**
- **1/2 cup kimchi juice**
- **1 cup cooked protein (chicken, pork, or tofu), diced**
- **1 carrot, finely diced**
- **1 cup frozen peas**
- **3 green onions, chopped**
- **2 tablespoons soy sauce**
- **1 tablespoon sesame oil**
- **1 tablespoon vegetable oil**
- **1 teaspoon sugar (optional)**
- **Sesame seeds and fried egg for topping (optional)**

INSTRUCTIONS

1. Heat vegetable oil in a large skillet or wok over medium heat.
2. Add diced carrots and frozen peas, stir-frying until they are tender.
3. Add chopped kimchi and cooked protein, sautéing for a few minutes.
4. Add rice to the skillet, breaking up any clumps and ensuring it mixes well with the other ingredients.
5. Pour in kimchi juice, soy sauce, and sesame oil. Stir to combine.
6. Taste and adjust the seasoning, adding sugar if desired.
7. Cook for an additional 5-7 minutes until the rice is heated through and slightly crispy.
8. Garnish with chopped green onions, sesame seeds, and a fried egg if desired.
9. Serve Kimchi Bokkeumbap hot, either as a standalone dish or as a side with additional Korean banchan.

Yubuchobap (Stuffed Tofu Pockets)

 4 servings   20 Mins   Kcal : 200 Fat: 6g carbs : 30g protein : 5g

Yubuchobap is a delightful Korean dish featuring tofu pockets filled with a seasoned mixture of rice and vegetables. It's a portable and tasty way to enjoy a balanced combination of flavors and textures.

INGREDIENTS

- **8 sheets of yubu (tofu skins)**
- **2 cups cooked short-grain rice**
- **1 cup julienned vegetables (carrots, cucumbers, and radishes)**
- **1/2 cup pickled yellow radish, julienned**
- **2 tablespoons soy sauce**
- **1 tablespoon sesame oil**
- **1 tablespoon mirin or rice wine**
- **1 tablespoon sesame seeds**
- **1 teaspoon sugar**
- **1 teaspoon minced garlic**
- **1 teaspoon grated ginger**
- **Chopped green onions for garnish**

INSTRUCTIONS

1. In a bowl, mix together cooked rice, julienned vegetables, pickled yellow radish, soy sauce, sesame oil, mirin, sesame seeds, sugar, minced garlic, and grated ginger.
2. Gently separate the yubu sheets and pat them dry with a paper towel.
3. Lay out each yubu sheet and place a spoonful of the rice mixture in the center.
4. Fold the sides of the yubu over the filling and roll it up, creating a pocket.
5. Repeat for all sheets.
6. Slice the stuffed tofu pockets into bite-sized pieces.
7. Garnish with chopped green onions.
8. Serve Yubuchobap as a flavorful and convenient snack or as part of a Korean-inspired lunchbox.

Kongnamul Muchim (Seasoned Soybean Sprouts)

 4 servings   15 Mins   Kcal : 40 Fat: 2g carbs : 5g protein : 3g

Kongnamul Muchim, or Seasoned Soybean Sprouts, is a classic Korean side dish known for its crunchy texture and savory flavor. This quick and easy recipe makes use of soybean sprouts, creating a delightful side dish that complements many Korean meals.

INGREDIENTS

- **4 cups soybean sprouts, washed and tails removed**
- **1 tablespoon soy sauce**
- **1 tablespoon sesame oil**
- **1 tablespoon sesame seeds**
- **1 teaspoon sugar**
- **1 teaspoon gochugaru (Korean red pepper flakes)**
- **2 cloves garlic, minced**
- **1 green onion, finely chopped**
- **Salt to taste**

INSTRUCTIONS

1. Bring a pot of water to a boil and blanch soybean sprouts for 3-5 minutes until they are slightly tender but still crisp. Drain and let them cool.
2. In a bowl, combine soy sauce, sesame oil, sesame seeds, sugar, gochugaru, minced garlic, and chopped green onions to create the seasoning mixture.
3. Add the cooled soybean sprouts to the bowl and toss them in the seasoning mixture until well coated.
4. Taste and adjust the seasoning if necessary, adding salt to your preference.
5. Serve Kongnamul Muchim as a refreshing side dish alongside rice and other Korean main courses. It's great for adding a crunchy element to your meal.

Patbingsu (Shaved Ice Dessert)

 4 servings   🕐 15 Mins   Kcal : 250   Fat: 6g   carbs : 45g   protein : 4g

Patbingsu is a popular Korean dessert that features finely shaved ice topped with a variety of sweet and colorful toppings. It's a refreshing and delightful treat, especially during the hot summer months.

INGREDIENTS

- **4 cups shaved ice (can use a shaved ice machine or crushed ice)**
- **1/2 cup sweetened red beans (canned or homemade)**
- **1/2 cup condensed milk or sweetened condensed milk**
- **1/2 cup chopped fruit (strawberries, kiwi, mango, etc.)**
- **1/4 cup mochi or rice cakes, cut into small pieces**
- **2 tablespoons sweetened adzuki beans or red bean paste**
- **2 tablespoons fruit preserves (such as strawberry or peach)**
- **2 tablespoons cornflakes or cereal for crunch (optional)**

INSTRUCTIONS

1. Shave ice into a fluffy texture using a shaved ice machine or crush ice in a blender.
2. Place the shaved ice in a bowl or dessert dish.
3. Arrange sweetened red beans, condensed milk, chopped fruit, mochi, sweetened adzuki beans, fruit preserves, and cornflakes on top of the shaved ice.
4. Serve immediately and enjoy the delightful combination of textures and flavors.

Kimchi Jjigae (Kimchi Stew)

 4 servings   40 Mins   Kcal : 300   Fat: 20gcarbs : 15g protein : 15g

Kimchi Jjigae is a robust and flavorful Korean stew made with fermented kimchi, pork, tofu, and vegetables.

INGREDIENTS

- 1 cup kimchi, chopped
- 200g pork belly, sliced
- block tofu, cubed
- 1 onion, sliced
- 2 cloves garlic, minced
- 1 tablespoon gochugaru (Korean red pepper flakes
- 1 tablespoon gochujang (Korean red pepper paste)
- 4 cups vegetable or beef broth
- Green onions for garnish

INSTRUCTIONS

1. In a pot, sauté pork belly until browned.
2. Add garlic, kimchi, and onions; stir-fry until fragrant.
3. Add gochugaru, gochujang, tofu, and broth.
4. Simmer until pork is cooked and flavors meld.
5. Garnish with green onions and serve hot.

Samgyeopsal (Korean Grilled Pork Belly)

 4 servings   20 Mins   Kcal : 250   Fat: 20gcarbs : 0gprotein : 15g

Samgyeopsal is a popular Korean BBQ dish featuring thick slices of pork belly grilled to perfection and enjoyed with dipping sauces.

INGREDIENTS

- **1 lb pork belly, thinly sliced**
- **Salt and pepper for seasoning**
- **Lettuce leaves for wrapping**
- **Ssamjang (Korean dipping sauce)**

INSTRUCTIONS

1. Season pork belly slices with salt and pepper.
2. Grill until crispy and cooked through.
3. Serve with lettuce leaves and ssamjang for wrapping.

Dak Bulgogi (Korean BBQ Chicken)

 4 servings   🕐 40 Mins   Kcal : 250 Fat: 15g carbs : 8g protein : 20g

Dak Bulgogi is a Korean grilled chicken dish marinated in a flavorful soy and sesame sauce, perfect for BBQ or stovetop cooking.

INGREDIENTS

- 1 lb chicken thighs, thinly sliced
- 1/4 cup soy sauce
- 2 tablespoons brown sugar
- 1 tablespoon sesame oil
- 1 tablespoon mirin
- 3 cloves garlic, minced
- 1 teaspoon ginger, grated
- Sesame seeds and green onions for garnish

INSTRUCTIONS

1. Mix soy sauce, brown sugar, sesame oil, mirin, garlic, and ginger to make the marinade.
2. Marinate chicken slices for at least 30 minutes.
3. Grill or pan-cook until chicken is fully cooked.
4. Garnish with sesame seeds and green onions before serving.

Korean Spicy Tofu (Dubu Jorim)

 4 servings   30 Mins   Kcal : 180   Fat: 12g   carbs : 8g   protein : 10g

Dubu Jorim is a spicy Korean tofu dish featuring pan-fried tofu simmered in a flavorful soy-based sauce.

INGREDIENTS

- 1 block firm tofu, cubed
- 2 tablespoons soy sauce
- 1 tablespoon gochugaru (Korean red pepper flakes)
- 1 tablespoon sesame oil
- 1 tablespoon sugar
- 2 cloves garlic, minced
- 1 teaspoon sesame seeds
- Green onions for garnish

INSTRUCTIONS

1. Pan-fry tofu cubes until golden brown on all sides.
2. In a bowl, mix soy sauce, gochugaru, sesame oil, sugar, and minced garlic.
3. Pour the sauce over the pan-fried tofu; simmer until sauce thickens.
4. Garnish with sesame seeds and chopped green onions.

The Asian Cookbook

Culinary Journeys Through China, Japan, Korea, and Thailand

By Lilly Unis

Made in the USA
Monee, IL
20 December 2023

50089885R00063